BRINGING JESUS TO THE DESERT

UNCOVER THE ANCIENT CULTURE, DISCOVER HIDDEN MEANINGS.

Ancient Context
Ancient Faith

Bringing Jesus to the Desert

Uncover the Ancient Culture, Discover Hidden Meanings.

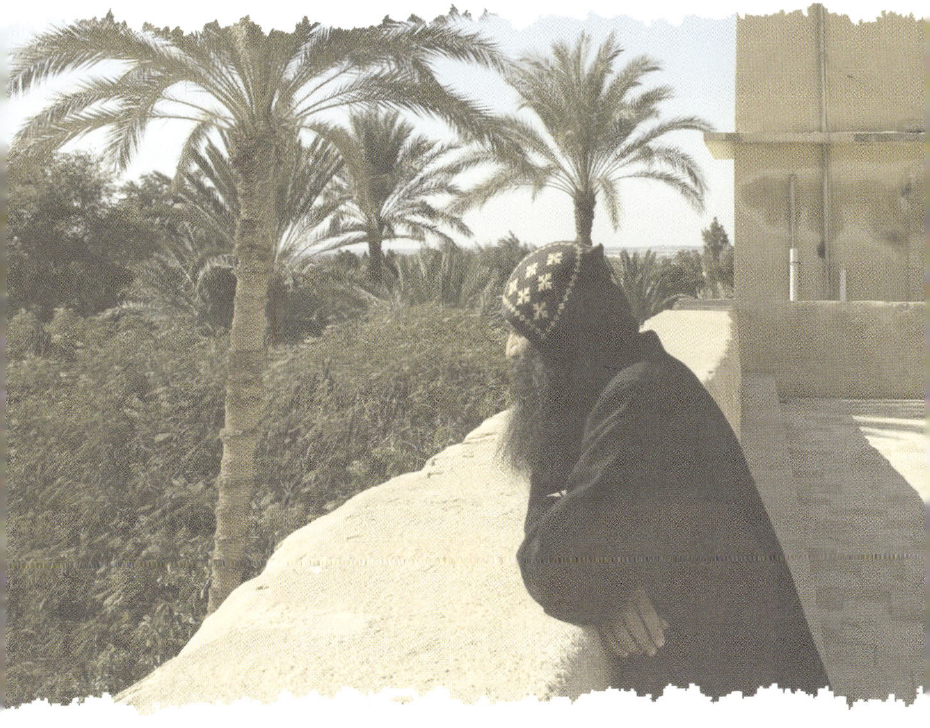

BRADLEY NASSIF

ZONDERVAN.com/
AUTHORTRACKER
follow your favorite authors

ZONDERVAN

Bringing Jesus to the Desert
Copyright © 2011 by Bradley L. Nassif

This title is also available as a Zondervan ebook.
Visit www.zondervan.com/ebooks.

Requests for information should be addressed to:

Zondervan, *Grand Rapids, Michigan* 49530

Library of Congress Cataloging-in-Publication Data

Nassif, Bradley.
 Bringing Jesus to the desert / Bradley Nassif.
   p. cm. — (Ancient context, ancient faith)
 Includes bibliographical references
 ISBN 978-0-310-31830-9 (softcover)
 1. Desert Fathers. I. Title.
BR67.N37 2011
 270.1092'2--dc22   2011007855

All Scripture quotations, unless otherwise indicated, are taken from the Holy Bible, *Today's New International Version®, TNIV®*. Copyright © 2001, 2005 by Biblica, Inc.™ Used by permission of Zondervan. All rights reserved worldwide.

Map by International Mapping. Copyright © 2012 by Zondervan. All rights reserved.

Any Internet addresses (websites, blogs, etc.) and telephone numbers in this book are offered as a resource. They are not intended in any way to be or imply an endorsement by Zondervan, nor does Zondervan vouch for the content of these sites and numbers for the life of this book.

All rights reserved. No part of this publication may be reproduced, stored in a retrieval system, or transmitted in any form or by any means — electronic, mechanical, photocopy, recording, or any other — except for brief quotations in printed reviews, without the prior permission of the publisher.

Cover photography: MATTES René / age fotostoc
Interior design: Kirk Douponce

Printed in China

For Melanie, my beloved daughter.
May their wisdom be yours.

Contents

	Series Introduction	9
1	**Holy Land, Holy People** Who Are the Desert Fathers and Mothers?	15
2	**Anthony of Egypt:** Patriarch of the Desert	37
3	**Makarios of Egypt:** Spirit-Bearer of Sketis	53
4	**Pachomius:** Community Builder of the Desert	71
5	**Melania:** Mother of the Mount of Olives	93
6	**Colorful Characters**	109
	John the Little	110
	Moses the Ethiopian	116
	Simeon the Stylite	120
	Conclusion Parting Thoughts	128

Series Introduction

ANCIENT CONTEXT, ANCIENT FAITH

EVERY COMMUNITY of Christians throughout history has framed its understanding of spiritual life within the context of its own culture. Byzantine Christians living in the fifth century and Puritan Christians living over a thousand years later used the world in which they lived to work out the principles of Christian faith, life, and identity. The reflex to build house churches, monastic communities, medieval cathedrals, steeple-graced and village-centered churches, or auditoriums with theater seating spring from the dominant cultural forces around believers.

Even the way we understand "faith in Christ" is to some degree shaped by these cultural forces. For instance, in the last three hundred years Western Christians have abandoned seeing faith as a chiefly communal exercise (this is not true in Africa or Asia). Among the many endowments of the European Enlightenment, individualism reigns supreme; Christian faith is a personal, private endeavor. We prefer to say, "I have accepted Christ as my Savior," rather than define ourselves through a *community* that follows Christ. Likewise (again, thanks to the Enlightenment), we have elevated rationalism as a premier value. Among many Christians faith is a construct of the mind, an effort at knowledge gained through study, an assent to a set of theological propositions. Sometimes even knowing *what you believe* trumps belief itself.

To be sure, many Christians today are challenging these Enlightenment assumptions and are seeking to chart a new path. Nevertheless, the new path charted is as much a by-product of modern cultural trends as any other feature. For example, we live today in a highly therapeutic society. Even if we are unaware of the discipline of psychology, we are still being shaped by values it has brought to our culture over the last hundred years. Faith today has an emotional, feeling-centered basis. Worship is measured by the emotive responses and the heart. The "felt needs" of a congregation shape many sermons.

Therefore, defining Christian faith as a personal choice based on well-informed convictions and inspired by emotionally engaging worship is a formula for spiritual formation that may be natural to us, but it has elements that are foreign to the experience of Christians in other cultures or other centuries. I imagine that fifth-century Christians would feel utterly lost in a modern church with its worship band and theater seating where lighting, sound, refreshments, and visual media are closely monitored. They might wonder if this *modern church* was chiefly indebted to the entertainment industry, like a tamed, baptized version of Rome's public arenas. They might also wonder how ten thousand people can gain any sense of shared life or community when each family comes and goes by car, lives long distances away, and barely recognizes the person sitting next to them.

THE ANCIENT LANDSCAPE

If it is true that *every* culture provides a framework in which the spiritual life is understood, the same must be said about the ancient world. The setting of Jesus and Paul in the Roman Empire was likewise shaped by cultural forces quite different from our own. And if we fail to understand these cultural forces, we will fail to understand many of the things Jesus and Paul taught.

This does not mean that the culture of the biblical world enjoys some sort of divine approval or endorsement. We do not need to imitate the biblical world in order to live a more biblical life. This was a culture that had its own preferences for dress, speech, diet, music, intellectual thought, religious expression, and personal identity. And their cultural values were no more significant than are our own. Modesty in antiquity was expressed in a way we may not understand. The arrangement of marriage partners would be foreign to our world of personal dating. Even how one prays (seated or standing, arms upraised or folded, aloud or silent) would have norms dictated by culture.

But if this is true—if cultural values are presupposed within every faithful community, both now and two thousand years ago—then the stories we read in the Bible may presuppose themes that are obscure to us. Moreover, when we read the Bible, we may misrepresent its message because we simply do not understand the cultural instincts of the first century. We live two thousand years distant; we live in the West and the ancient Middle East is not native territory for us.

INTERPRETING FROM AFAR

This means we must be cautious interpreters of the Bible. We need to be careful lest we presuppose that *our cultural instincts* are the same as those represented in the Bible. We need to be *culturally aware* of our own place in time—and we must work to comprehend the cultural context of the Scriptures that we wish to understand. Too often interpreters have lacked cultural awareness when reading the Scriptures. We have failed to recognize the gulf that exists between our present-day situation and the context of the Bible. We have forgotten that we read the Bible as foreigners, as visitors who have traveled not only to a new geography but to a new century. We are literary tourists who are deeply in need of a guide.

The goal of this series is to be such a guide—to explore themes from the biblical world that are often misunderstood. In what sense, for instance, did the physical geography of Israel shape its people's sense of spirituality? How did the storytelling of Jesus presuppose cultural themes now lost to us? What celebrations did Jesus know intimately (such as a child's birth, a wedding, or a burial)? What agricultural or religious festivals did he attend? How did he use common images of labor or village life or social hierarchy when he taught? Did he use humor or allude to politics?

In many cases—just as in our world—the more delicate matters are handled indirectly, and it takes expert guidance to revisit their correct meaning. In a word, this series employs *cultural anthropology, archaeology,* and *contextual backgrounds* to open up new vistas for the Christian reader. And if the average reader suddenly sees a story or an idea in a new way, if a familiar passage is suddenly opened for new meaning and application, then this effort has succeeded.

This is the fourth book in the Ancient Context, Ancient Faith series. In previous books we explored how the biblical world shaped the spirituality of those who lived within it. We examined the cultural landscape, the parables of Jesus, and encounter stories where Jesus transformed the lives of individuals.

I was delighted when Dr. Bradley Nassif agreed to write this volume because it is an area of technical knowledge that frankly requires a specialized expert—and Dr. Nassif is such a scholar. Following the New Testament era, Christians wanted to return to the Middle Eastern deserts in order to recreate a spirituality shaped by the cultural forces that influenced Jesus and his followers.

While an indigenous Middle Eastern church from Syria to Egypt flourished in these regions, we know little of their everyday life. However, another fascinating movement was born that we know a great deal about. Christian leaders entered the desert wastelands of Syria, Palestine, and Egypt and there explored a spirituality foreign to us today. In many cases, they returned from the desert as saints. Their experiences and writings resonate closely with the biblical world, and from their teachings we can learn a great deal. Dr. Nassif will be our guide through this terrain. Not only is he a Middle Easterner himself, but he has built his career studying these very movements from antiquity.

Gary M. Burge, Series Editor
Wheaton, Illinois

Chapter 1

Holy Land, Holy People: Who Are the Desert Fathers and Mothers?

IN THE wilderness of Judea is an ancient road from Jerusalem to Jericho. There, nestled in the rocky mountainside, is the ancient Monastery of St. George. The monastery is surrounded by towering mountains. A hermit built it in AD 480. The tradition of the monastery tells us that the prophet Elijah stayed in that area while on his way to Mount Sinai (1 Kings 19:1–9) after he had prayed fire down from heaven to defeat Baal, the false god of King Ahab. Ahab's wife, Jezebel, pledged to kill him. Even though he saw God's power at work, he fled for his life to Mount Horeb. On his way he stopped here, in the wilderness of Judea, where under a broom bush he prayed that he might die. Fear, doubt, and despair overtook him.

For centuries, the Monastery of St. George has commemorated the memory of St. Elijah. His story calls us to ponder our

Broom bush

own journey with God. Like Elijah, we too have seen God's power in our lives. Yet in times of trouble we doubt God's care for us. This is a sacred place where we meet ourselves in the life of Elijah. We remember how easy it is to lose faith, even when God has manifested his presence so powerfully in our lives.

The Land and Pilgrimage

The Bible lands have always been a unique and powerful place for spiritual transformation. Pilgrims across the centuries have

Monastery of St. George

traveled to Jerusalem and its surrounding lands to see the sacred places where the stories of the Old Testament happened and where Jesus Christ lived and taught. Ancient Christians since the fourth century erected entire monasteries to honor the special sites where Jesus taught and ministered.

These monastic Christians living in the Holy Land provided pilgrims with a physical link to the Old Testament prophets, John the Baptist, and

Icon of St. Elijah ascending to heaven on a fiery chariot. The Monastery of St. George commemorates St. Elijah.

People visiting the Western Wall in Jerusalem. Pilgrims across the centuries have discovered how great saints turned the Holy Land into a land of holy people.

Chapter One, Holy Land, Holy People 17

the apostles. They were living legacies of the continuing story of the biblical world. The monks of the Bible lands saw themselves as protectors of a biblical culture and message that had lived on in their own day. They believed that in this land, God himself had become human in Jesus Christ, who worked miracles, died for our sins, and victoriously rose from the dead. It was the place where God walked on earth.

This book tells the forgotten stories of ancient Christians of the Middle East. They are known in history as the Desert Fathers (*abbas*) and Mothers (*ammas*). These were great men and women of the Middle East who colonized the deserts of Palestine, Syria, and Egypt from the third to sixth centuries for the sake of the gospel. *This book is the story of how the Desert Fathers and Mothers turned the Holy Land into a land of holy people.*

Is There Really a "Holy Land"?

Before looking at the relationship between the land and biblical culture, we need to recognize that some modern Christians do not like to speak of particular places as "Holy Land" or spiritually significant. They are wary of the idea of "sacred space." True worship, they say, is not linked to particular places but is a matter of worshiping God "in the Spirit and in truth" (John 4:24). This seems also to have been one of the views of the church during the first three centuries. Yet we also know that early Christians celebrated communion annually over the sacred gravesites of martyrs.

ICON OF THE MARTYRDOM OF ST. IGNATIUS.

In the fourth century, however, a major change entered the church after the triumph of Christianity over the Roman Empire. Though fourth-century church fathers like Gregory Nyssa maintained the earlier view, others like Basil and Cyril of Jerusalem disagreed. Yet the Desert Fathers and Mothers remind us that a disembodied faith can be anemic because spiritual life is physically rooted in the incarnation. And Palestine is the only place on earth where God became human. Although there is nothing magically spiritual about the places where Jesus walked, the land could inspire godliness in a unique way. They argued, however, that just being in the Holy Land is not enough. Living a godly life there is what is praiseworthy.

The Land and Culture

As we will see, there is a direct link between the wilderness experience of these early desert Christians and the biblical story of the desert found in the Old and New Testaments. The great *abbas* and *ammas* of the desert lived, thought, breathed, acted, and participated in Middle Eastern culture. Theirs was

MONASTERY OF ST. SABAS

a Middle Eastern spirituality forged in the very setting known to Moses and Jesus—a setting that was as severe as it was inspiring.

Some of their monasteries and churches have survived hundreds of years into the modern world. The Monastery of St. Sabas (*Mar Saba*) near Jerusalem has been occupied almost continuously since the fifth century. Now, as then, these Christians possess a vibrant spiritual and cultural continuity with the Bible lands. Today there are over ten million Arabic-speaking Christians who draw deeply from the spiritual wells of this rich biblical and monastic heritage. Their churches and monasteries have blossomed in the heartland of the biblical world of the Middle East.[1]

But most of us in the West have forgotten about them. In fact, many have never even heard of them. For us, these ancient desert dwellers are marginal figures of the past. Their names are foreign to our Christian vocabulary. Most of us know of Augustine, Thomas Aquinas, John of the Cross, Theresa of Avila, Bernard of Clairvaux, Martin Luther, John Calvin, and other great leaders of the West. Some may well have heard about Anthony the Great, but what of Pachomius, Makarios of Egypt, Simeon the Stylite, Melania, John the Little, Moses the Ethiopian, and other desert dwellers we will meet in this book? If we know them at all, they appear as social dropouts, exiles from life—people who are culturally irrelevant to the modern world.

Nothing could be further from the truth. Their contemporary relevance is staggering. In the Desert Fathers and Mothers we discover a vibrant spiritual life that our modern world so desperately longs for. As we will see, their eccentric way of life in the desert was partly a response to the church's

LUSH LAND OF CANAAN CONTRASTS WITH THE DESERT WILDERNESS

spiritual poverty, the poverty of love. They protested that lack of knowledge was not the central problem of the church; the real problem was the poverty of love. Compared to them, our love for God and neighbor is also virtually bankrupt today. The intensity of love's "holy fire" has died down to a mere flicker. Perhaps that is why, they argued, the core battleground of our earthly pilgrimage is the human heart.[2]

There is a direct connection between their concerns and the subjects explored in this series of books on Ancient Context, Ancient Faith. As we saw in volume 1 (*The Bible and the Land*), the biblical theme of "land and pilgrimage" is perhaps the most important one in all Scripture. The Bible juxtaposes the promised land and the wilderness as a supreme metaphor for the life of the believer. The desert is portrayed as the place where we learn the most about God. It is a spiritual mentor. The Christians we will meet in this volume are some of the desert's greatest teachers who have ever lived.

We learned in volume 2 (*Jesus, the Middle Eastern Storyteller*) how skilled teachers in Jesus' day could spin a good tale. Jesus himself was a master storyteller. He communicated the gospel by using word pictures, dramatic actions, metaphors, and stories. Almost one third of his teachings were given in parables. He lived in a world where literacy was rare and books were rarer still. Communication was oral and memorization was common. In the same way, most of the Desert Fathers and Mothers were illiterate people. They lived in a society in which only 3 percent of the population could read and write. The greatest number of people were peasants, shepherds, camel traders, former slaves, prostitutes, and other social outcasts. These teaching techniques of the Middle East did not die out with Jesus, as some scholars have imagined. In the period following Jesus, we have over two thousand stories told by Jewish rabbis, whose methods were often identical with those of Jesus.

There were also Arab storytellers in the Middle East. Some of the most masterful ones were the monks of Palestine, Syria, Lebanon, and Egypt. Like Jesus, they rarely (if ever) used technical, theological speech with their audiences. Rather, they preferred to use simple stories, sayings, and enacted parables to drive home a memorable saying or to impart an

JESUS USES THE PARABLE OF THE SHEEP AND THE GOATS. EARLY MONKS ALSO USED STORIES AND PARABLES TO SPREAD THEIR MESSAGES.

insightful truth about the spiritual life. They taught with wit and wisdom. Knowing how slow and stubborn we humans can be when it comes to changing our lives, they sometimes used subtle humor to get past the defenses of their disciples in order to instill a sidesplitting word of wisdom that would be forever implanted in their memory. (See the hilarious story in chapter 3 of how St. Makarios of Egypt used a cemetery to teach a disciple how to die to the praises and insults of others.)

Why the Desert?

The story of the Desert Fathers and Mothers begins with the Bible itself. They based their lives on a distinct theology of the desert found on the pages of the Old and New Testaments. For example, the Old Testament speaks of Moses, who went up on a mountain forty days and forty nights to receive God's revelation of the covenant (Ex. 24:18). The children of Israel later wandered in the wilderness for forty years under Moses "to humble and test you [Israel] in order to know what was in your heart, whether or not you would keep his commands" (Deut. 8:2). Later prophets such as Elijah (1 Kings 19) lived in the desert as they warned the Israelites to forsake their wor-

John the Baptist

ship of false gods. On the Day of Atonement (Lev. 16), the high priest laid the sins of Israel on the head of a scapegoat and sent it into the wilderness as a sign of repentance and God's forgiveness.

In the New Testament, the greatest of all prophets, John the Baptist, lived a celibate life of self-denial that moved later generations of Christians to follow his example. Dressed in camel's hair and a leather belt, John practiced an austere diet of eating insects and wild honey. There, in the desert, he called people to repent as he announced the coming kingdom of God (Matt. 3:1–12).

Jesus himself "was led by the Spirit into the wilderness to be tempted by the devil" (Matt. 4:1). His fast of forty days and nights recalled the experiences of Moses, Elijah, and the forty years of Israel's temptation in the wilderness. Jesus later declared that some disciples would be "eunuchs . . . who made themselves eunuchs for the sake of the kingdom of heaven" (Matt. 19:12 NASB). He defined discipleship as a daily dying to one's own will: "Whoever wants to be my disciple must deny themselves and take up their cross daily and follow me. For whoever wants to save their life will lose it, but whoever loses their life for me will save it" (Luke 9:23). Some would even have to give up all their earthly possessions. To the rich young ruler Jesus commanded: "Sell everything you have and give to the

Aerial view of the traditional location of Jesus' temptation.

poor, and you will have treasure in heaven. Then come, follow me" (Luke 18:22).

These and other biblical texts inspired later generations of believers to take up their cross and follow Jesus in a radical form of Christian discipleship. By the fourth century, the monastic movement began in earnest. Christians in large numbers responded to the gospel by leaving the cities and going into the desert regions. Their movement was a response to Christ's call, but it was also a reaction to the growing worldliness of the church that occurred under Emperor Constantine (AD 312–337).

Constantine was the first Roman emperor to become a Christian. He outlawed imperial persecutions against Christians and began supporting the church by commissioning copies of the Bible, building churches, changing unjust laws against slaves, and even protecting the faith against heresies by convening the Council of Nicea in AD 325. This new alliance between church and state created an awkward relationship that neither side was fully prepared to handle.

In time, large numbers of people joined the church for the social privileges it brought. Many sought status and prosperity more than the cross. Christians became so comfortable that they forgot about the return of Christ and the coming

Constantine became the first Christian ruler of Rome. After stopping the persecution of Christians, the church swelled in large numbers. The monastic movement partly arose in reaction to the growing worldliness of the church.

judgment. The growth of nominal Christianity made the church a spiritually sick institution. The gospel had become too acculturated with the Roman Empire. Radical illnesses called for radical remedies. Ordinary men and women who heard Christ's call to take up the cross responded by fleeing to the desert. This way of life became a form of martyrdom in which

Council of Nicea

they died daily to their own wills and desires. It was a totally spontaneous movement led by laypeople, not by the clergy.

There were basically three forms of monastic life. The fewest number of monks lived alone (called hermits, anchorites, or hesychasts); most lived in a community (called cenobites); still others combined the hermit and community lifestyles into a middle way, spending part of their week alone and the rest in church with others (on weekends). All groups gathered around one or several elders. Even the hermits occasionally left their dwellings to obtain counsel from a spiritual elder who was wiser in the faith.

The monastic movements in Egypt, Palestine, Syria, and Asia Minor had their own unique but interrelated histories. They were not, properly speaking, monks of the late medieval or modern worlds. They did not live in massive stone buildings with quiet cloisters, even though some of them outwardly looked similar. In Egypt, men and women fled the cities to take up residence along the banks of the River Nile, in remote caves, at abandoned forts, in tombs, and on mountaintops. Most other regions did the same, depending on their local geographies and terrains.

By the end of the fourth century, thousands of hermits and monastic settlements flourished in the region. To the early

MONASTERY OF ST. GEORGE AND THE SURROUNDING JUDEAN WILDERNESS

Remote caves in which some monks would take residence.

Christians, these holy men and women were "the salt of the earth" and "the light of the world" (Matt. 5:13–16). They refused to succumb to the world, the flesh, and the devil (cf. 1 John 2:15–17). Like their biblical counterparts, the monks served as a prophetic reminder that the kingdom of God is not of this world.

Ironically, the greatest of these humble monks wielded enormous power in the ancient world. Their reputation for

Some desert dwellers lived in lush areas near the Nile River.

humility and holiness inspired crowds of pilgrims to flock to remote regions of the desert. The poor and needy, as well as emperors, generals, and politicians, would travel long distances by foot or donkey just to see the face of one of these elders or obtain a word of wisdom and healing. The Holy Land had truly become a land of holy people.

Holy Land, Holy Heart

Life in the desert meant something totally opposite of what we are inclined to think it was. The desert was a place of death, testing, repentance, and spiritual warfare. It was not a place of escape as much as a place of countercultural engagement. It was not a retreat but the frontlines of spiritual warfare. It is a place where the victory of Christ over sin, death, and the devil was proclaimed, fought, and won. Under the power of the risen Lord, it is where the heart was purified, the passions conquered, sin destroyed, and humanity renewed.

The monks practiced a way of life that was shaped by the terrain in which they lived. The outward physical realities of the desert matched the inward spiritual realities of their hearts. The very nature of the barren land supported a path of self-denial that the monks called *asceticism.* It fostered a life of detachment from the material things of this world. The

Judean wilderness

A Coptic monk meditating in the desert of Wadi Natrun, Egypt.

wilderness encouraged the monk to slow down and let things go. Its dry and barren land required one to learn survival skills. The monk had to know what to keep and what to let go of in order to stay alive. Simplicity was the essence of survival.

As a place of profound silence, the land beckoned the invitation of the psalmist to "be still, and know that I am God" (Ps. 46:10). The silence of the great Judean and Egyptian deserts could be absolutely immense. The desert invited the monks to enter into that inner space of "being" rather than "doing." Silence created space for listening to God. The vast emptiness of the terrain created a place of inner peace. There was no place for the monks to hide.

The desert fostered a radical honesty that stripped the monks of all pretentions. It invited them to embrace the limits of their own humanity. It called them to take a good hard look at themselves so they could begin wrestling with the demons and their inner passions. In short, the desert was an expansive place that whittled people down to size.

The Quest for True Love

The goal of the monastic life was partly disclosed in the term *monk*, which comes from a Greek word meaning "to live alone." The title indicates not just a lifestyle but also the purpose of a monk's life. Above all else, theirs was a life that sought God, and God alone. That is why they declared a virtual war on the inner adversaries that hid secretly in their hearts, and they were watchful of their stealth attacks (Prov. 4:23). They concentrated their energies on the source of their problems, the inner person—its selfish orientation, dark impulses, sexual preoccupations, greed, lust, anger, unforgiveness, hatred, and other "works of the flesh" (Gal. 5:19–21 NRSV).

The Desert Fathers and Mothers knew that every believer had within them a powerful attraction to sin. That is why they engaged in the hard work of holiness, something they called *askçsis*, or spiritual training. The transformation of the mind—or *nous*, as they called it—into the mind of Christ was the lifelong object of their efforts. The monks rose or fell on the quality of their inner thoughts and choices (Rom. 12:1–2; 2 Cor. 3:18; Phil. 4:8). Evil thoughts (*ponçroi logismoi*) were the greatest enemy of the spiritual life.

At the heart of their training was repentance. They were convinced that their inner natures were so out of sync with God's will that nothing but a strong dose of his grace could fix them. Only repentance could clear away the stony rubble of their hearts before God's grace could take root and grow. Repentance was a lifestyle for them, not a single event.

Athanasius, the biographer of Anthony of Egypt, wrote, "God became humanized so that humans might become divinized" (my trans.).[3] The term early Christians used to describe this divinization was *theôsis*. Through baptism, the

ICON OF ST. ATHANASIUS

CHAPTER ONE, HOLY LAND, HOLY PEOPLE 31

Eucharist, church life, and works of service, the monks sought to become by grace what Christ was by nature: fully human and fully divine. The Christlikeness they sought, however, was not one that could impart creative powers or make them to become fourth persons of the Trinity. That would have been blasphemous to them. Rather, they believed they could not be truly godly unless they were first truly human. And they could not be truly human unless they were in communion with Christ in his Trinitarian relations.

Modern writer Darrell Johnson has described this Trinitarian love life well in his book *Experiencing the Trinity*: "At the center of the universe there is a relationship.... It is *out* of that relationship that we were created and redeemed, and it is *for* that relationship we were created and redeemed."[4] That is what the monks were all about: love for God and love for neighbor (Mark 12:29–31) through union with Christ.

Some of us may wonder why it was so important for them (and us) to enter into the inner life of the Holy Trinity. The short answer is this: because a right understanding of God is foundational to personal holiness and ministry. If Jesus is not "one with the Father," they reasoned, we are still in our sins, for the one who died on the cross was then incapable of being the mediator between God and man. That is one reason why St. Athanasius, an ardent defender of the divinity of Christ, wrote the *Life of Anthony*. Nothing short of the fully divine Son of God could account for the great holiness of a man like Anthony of Egypt.

Also the monks' baptism was done in the name of the Holy Trinity (Matt. 28:19). The monks sought to live out their baptism by dying daily to their own wills and rising with Christ to walk in newness of life (Rom. 6:11–12). The spiritual atmosphere in which they lived was the very life of the Trinitarian God. Prayer itself was a Trinitarian experience. It was the supreme manifestation of their baptismal and monastic vocation. The desert dwellers knew that Scripture taught them to "pray continually" (1 Thess. 5:17). This was made possible by the Father (Matt. 6:6) through the Son (John 16:24) in the Holy Spirit (Jude 20).

Ultimately, love—the Trinitarian love of God—was the reason why the monks took up their crosses to fashion the old creation into the new in the desert. Unlike the worldly values of their contemporaries (and ours), they offered an alternative portrait of what being human really means. When practiced in humility, their ascetic rigor resulted in greater love. The monks fasted because they were hungry to love God more; they prayed because they wanted closer communion with God and neighbor; they contemplated so they could better fix their gaze on their divine spouse; they practiced silence because they wanted to hear God in order to speak and act more wisely to the people around them. The goal of every spiritual practice was love.

In the chapters that follow, we will travel to the far regions of the desert to visit some of the most revered Christians who ever graced the earth. We cannot tell their entire stories; rather, we can give only the highlights. As we profile their lives and survey their teachings, we will discover lost spiritual treasures for which our modern world hungers. We will see the direct link that still exists between the desert experience of the great *abbas* and *ammas* of the Middle East and the biblical story of the desert found in the Old and New Testaments.

The people and places we will survey have their own regional characteristics and local heroes. The Egyptian monks became the most famous of all in Christian antiquity. The chapters on Sts. Anthony of Egypt, Pachomius, and Makarios are a few of the most renowned we will meet from that tradition. There are a large number of female monks (nuns) and eccentric men who were hugely popular in their day, but we know precious little about them. One woman we do know about is St. Melania the Younger, whom we will write about in chapter 5. In chapter 6, we will gather three biographies in one essay titled "Colorful Characters." Here we will meet Sts. John the Little, Moses the Ethiopian, and Simeon the Stylite.

In addition to secondary sources noted throughout the book, the major original writings I have used are *The Life of Anthony* by St. Athanasius[5] and *Sayings of the Desert Fathers*.[6] The latter is a collection of stories and sayings of 131 heroes of the desert arranged in alphabetical order, copied perhaps in the sixth century. These sayings and stories capture the imagination and powerfully speak to the world of the modern reader. *Sayings of the Desert Fathers* became widely popular for spiritual direction in Christian antiquity. It is my hope that readers will soon buy this book and its companion, *The Desert Fathers: Sayings of Early Christian Monks*, and use them as a travel companion for their own spiritual journeys. I keep mine at my bedside and refer to them often for inspiration and guidance.

Now it's time for us to start our journey through the Middle East. So pack your bags, grab your canteen, and mount your camel. We are about to take an imaginary trip back in time. Our first stop will be in the land of Egypt. There, in the next chapter, we will meet the "Father of Monasticism," Anthony the Great, who became the enduring model by which all subsequent monks would pattern their lives. As we will see, his words are more than mere sayings; they are life-giving truths of a Middle Eastern peasant whose simple wisdom stretched back to the very days of Jesus.

Chapter 2

ANTHONY OF EGYPT: PATRIARCH OF THE DESERT

MIDDLE EASTERN culture is a family affair. Each clan prides itself on in its ancestral history. My grandfather is a case in point. He immigrated to America from Lebanon in the early twentieth century. All his children, grandchildren, and great-grandchildren now have him to thank for their citizenship. He was the patriarch of the family, physically and spiritually.

I keep a picture of my grandfather (*JID-ee*, as we say in Arabic) hanging in our dining room so we'll remember our roots and imitate his faith. The old sepia photo captures the spirit of the man when it was taken in 1929. In it he's wearing a black handlebar mustache and is dressed in a simple brown suit and tie with hands clasped behind his back as he stands upright in a posture that bespeaks a confident faith.

Whenever we look at his picture and reminisce about the kind of man he was, we feel inspired to imitate his faith. Everyone who knew him—brothers, sisters, children, and grandchildren across the generations—passed down stories and sayings from his life that endeared our memory of him. His

MONASTERY OF ST. ANTHONY
© Chris Bradley/www.agefotostock.com

PHOTO OF GRANDFATHER FRANK FERRIS IN 1937 AFTER IMMIGRATING FROM LEBANON TO WICHITA, KANSAS. AS ANTHONY OF EGYPT WAS THE PATRIARCH OF THE DESERT, SO FRANK WAS THE SPIRITUAL FATHER OF THE FERRIS CLAN.

FERRIS HADDAD, THE FATHER OF FRANK FERRIS, LIVED IN THE TINY MOUNTAIN VILLAGE OF M'HAITHE NEAR BEIRUT, LEBANON. HE WAS A VERY GENEROUS MAN, A LAY PREACHER IN THE VILLAGE, AND LIVED TO BE AROUND 100. FATHER AND SON BOTH DIED IN A MANNER LIKE SOME OF THE DESERT FATHERS WE READ ABOUT IN THE "SAYINGS OF THE DESERT FATHERS." THEY SAID THEY HAD BEEN VISITED BY AN ANGEL WHO TOLD THEM THEY WOULD DIE IN A CERTAIN NUMBER OF DAYS. ON THE APPOINTED DAY, FERRIS GATHERED HIS FAMILY AROUND HIM, ASKED EACH FOR FORGIVENESS, KISSED THEM GOODBYE, AND THEN DIED. THE PHOTO WAS APPARENTLY TAKEN IN DAMASCUS.

children reminisce about how Grandfather attended church faithfully. They saw him pray and read his Bible in Arabic every afternoon.

A famous saying came during his observance of Great Lent one year. In the Eastern Orthodox Church, Lent is a forty-day period of strenuous fasting and self-denial in preparation for Easter. It's easy to become legalistic at that time of year by comparing your own level of fasting with that of someone else. But Grandfather understood it more deeply than most. He told his daughter, "God wants us to fast not only from food, but to fast from here (touching his lips) so that we do not judge, gossip, or speak evil of others."

During the days of the Great Depression, a tender story of faith is told about a divine visitation he experienced. One day an old man with a beard came to the door of his house begging for food. Grandfather immediately welcomed him to the table for dinner. Shortly after the meal, Grandfather and Grandmother were washing the dishes. When they turned around to talk to the stranger who had been sitting at the table, he was suddenly gone. They were so startled Grandfather ran outside, but the guest was nowhere to be found. He returned to the house and said to his wife, "God brought something good to us today, Mary. We fed one of his angels" (see Heb. 13:2: "Do not forget to show hospitality to strangers, for by so doing some people have shown hospitality to angels without knowing it").

When it came time for Grandfather to die, God prepared him for it in a dream. A few days later he was gone.

THE EXTENT OF ANTHONY'S INFLUENCE

These are just a few examples of how a Middle Eastern family remembers their patriarch's life of faith. In exactly the same way, Anthony of Egypt (AD 251–356) is remembered as "the father of Christian monasticism." He is the honored patriarch of the entire monastic family in the ancient world. Everyone who took up the monastic life knew of him and modeled their lives after the sayings and stories about him that were passed down from generation to generation. His biography, *The Life of Anthony*, was

SAINT ANTHONY THE HERMIT. (CHURCH OF THE VIRGIN, ASSINOU, CYPRUS, 1105-06).

second only to the Bible in popularity in the early and medieval church. It was the equivalent of being on *The New York Times* bestsellers list for over a thousand years.

Before we take a closer look at Anthony's life and teaching, it's important that we understand how enormous this one man's influence was. The impact of his life in both Western and Eastern Christianity has been incalculable. By the middle of the fourth century his withdrawal into the desert had produced such notoriety that his biographer, Athanasius, asked, "How is that he is heard of in Spain, Gaul, Rome and Africa, even though he is concealed and sitting in a mountain...?"[7] The learned St. Augustine, one of the greatest Western theologians of all time, attributed his own conversion to the influence of this illiterate Egyptian peasant.[8]

In the Eastern Orthodox tradition, Anthony has continued to impact the spiritual culture of Russia, Romania, Greece, and every other country where the Orthodox Church thrived. Some sayings and stories of Anthony, along with those of other desert dwellers in this book, were eventually preserved and transmitted in *The Philokalia*. Next to the Bible, it is the most widely read book in the Orthodox world today.[9]

Even today, the legacy of Anthony's life remains. St. Anthony's Monastery (*Deir Mar Antonios*), possibly the world's oldest

ST. ANTHONY'S MONASTERY IN EGYPT.

monastic settlement, still exists. It was founded in 356 shortly after Anthony died. Hidden deep in the Red Sea Mountains where Anthony once lived, it consists of a self-contained village with a community of monks who practice a way of life that has hardly changed in 1,600 years. In Orthodox churches, Anthony's memory is commemorated every January 17 with the following liturgical poetry:

> *You became like the zealous Elijah in his way of life; you followed John the Baptist in his upright ways and became a dweller in the wilderness.... O righteous Anthony, when you put away worldly troubles you spent your life in solitude and silence, becoming in all ways like John the Baptist. Therefore with John we honor you, O father of fathers, Antony.*[10]

LIFE OF ANTHONY THE GREAT

Anthony was born in 251 in the village of Coma in southern Egypt from moderately wealthy parents. He lived contentedly in his home as an obedient child. Nearly every Sunday he went to church and took to heart the Scripture readings that were read aloud. Shortly after his parents died, when he was around twenty years old, Anthony went to church and heard the words of Jesus to the rich young ruler about detachment from worldly possessions: "Go, sell everything you have and give to the poor.... Then come, follow me" (Mark 10:21). He took these words literally as a personal command from God and in obedience sold all his property and gave it to the poor. Anthony deeply desired to be a doer of the word, not merely a hearer (cf. James 1:22).

Anthony Becomes an Ascetic

From that point on, Anthony lived an "ascetic" lifestyle. An ascetic is a spiritual athlete. It's a person who denies himself excessive food, drink, sleep, and other physical pleasures that soften our lives whenever we allow ourselves to indulge in them. Anthony did not hate his body or other material blessings God has given us in creation, but he only allowed himself to enjoy these things to the extent that they did not hinder him from growing closer to God. He adopted severe austerities for his life in order to foster growth into the image and likeness of Jesus

Christ[11] through the renewal of his mind. To protect himself from deadly legalism, Anthony always used spiritual discernment and love for God as the guiding goals of his ascetic life.

Armed with an attitude of obedience and self-denial, Anthony began his new life by living with an old hermit near the outskirts of his hometown. Like a sponge, he soaked up every lesson he could learn from the old hermit. With God as his trainer, Anthony pursued an ascetic life of work, prayer, and Scripture memory. "He prayed constantly.... For he paid such close attention to what was read that nothing from Scripture did he fail to take in—rather he grasped everything, and in him the memory took the place of books."[12]

Anthony then sought the company of other hermits who were living solitary lives in nearby villages. He was not content merely to observe their way of life; he wanted to integrate their virtues into his own character. Athanasius wrote that Anthony "was sincerely obedient to those men of zeal he visited" and put into practice the virtues of each. One man was exceptionally gracious, another eager for prayer, another free from anger, while others prayed, fasted, slept on the ground, or were patient, studious, or gentle. "And

JOHN CLIMACUS, ALSO KNOWN AS ST. JOHN OF THE LADDER, WAS A 7TH-CENTURY MONK AND ABBOT OF ST. CATHERINE'S MONASTERY NEAR MT. SINAI. THIS ICON DEPICTS HIS MASTERFUL WORK TITLED "THE LADDER OF DIVINE ASCENT." JOHN SAID, "WHEN WE DIE, WE WILL NOT BE CRITICIZED FOR HAVING FAILED TO WORK MIRACLES. WE WILL NOT BE ACCUSED OF HAVING FAILED TO BE THEOLOGIANS OR CONTEMPLATIVES. BUT WE WILL CERTAINLY HAVE SOME EXPLANATION TO OFFER TO GOD FOR NOT HAVING MOURNED UNCEASINGLY."

having been filled in this manner, he returned to his own place of discipline ... gathering the attributes of each in himself, and striving to manifest in himself what was best from all."[13]

Anthony Lives in a Tomb and Fort

Anthony spent the next twenty years living in more or less complete seclusion. Hardly anyone saw him or talked with him during those years of silence. His solitude began around the age of thirty-five, when he left home and took up residence in a rocky tomb that had been carved out in a mountainside away from his village. This was strange by anyone's account, but shortly we'll see why he lived in a place that symbolized death. Later he went even further into the desert, where he lived in an abandoned fort at a place called Outer Mountain (Pispir) on the Nile River in southern Egypt. There he put together a loosely organized colony of disciples under his leadership.

During his time Anthony engaged in intense spiritual warfare. Athanasius tells us that he was constantly harassed by demons, physically beaten by the devil, and tempted with fornication and other foul thoughts. "Nearly twenty years he spent in this manner pursuing the ascetic life by

Hunting birds in the marshes with a net (Thebes, 1420 - 1411 BC). Abba Anthony said, "I saw the snares that the enemy spreads out over the world and I groaned to myself saying, 'What can get me through such snares?' Then I heard a voice saying to me, 'Humility.'"

CHAPTER TWO, ANTHONY OF EGYPT

himself, not venturing out and only occasionally being seen by anyone."[14] It's difficult to know whether these struggles involved actual physical encounters with demons or just vivid descriptions of psychological battles. Both may well have occurred.

How did Anthony survive the vicious attacks on his body and soul? In one of the most famous sayings in all the desert literature, Anthony described the weapon needed to win the battle: "Abba Anthony said, 'I saw the snares that the enemy spreads out over the world and I groaned to myself saying, "What can get me through such snares?" Then I heard a voice saying to me, "Humility." ' "[15]

The Desert as Womb and Tomb of the Spiritual Life

A familiar theme emerges in the context of Anthony's spiritual warfare. It's a biblical message we've read about over and over in other volumes of this series and in the introduction to this book, namely, that the desert is a paradoxical wasteland where life and death coexist.

It's hard for us to understand why Anthony would live alone for twenty years in a tomb and an abandoned fort in the barren wastelands of Egypt. Let's be honest. It's a pretty weird and morbid way of living the Christian life. The thought of a person actually living in a grave is as shocking to us as it was in Anthony's day.

COPTIC MONK PRAYING IN ORIGINAL CAVE OF ST. ANTHONY.

The answer to this perplexing riddle is not hard to find when we see how Anthony associated the physical desert with its spiritual lessons. In short, the desert became a womb and tomb for Anthony. He lived in a physical realm that literally encouraged him to die daily to the world, the flesh, and the devil. We saw this in the desert experiences of biblical leaders in the first volume of this series.[16] Those same biblical themes lived on in Middle Eastern culture and became radically embodied in the life of this simple hermit. The biblical message and Anthony's message are one and the same: the desert is a place where faith is tested, repentance is made, and the heart is renewed. Anthony's tomb and fort make this abundantly clear in a dramatic way.

Anthony's tomb can still be seen today. The tomb is made of sandstone that was carved out from the side of a mountain. On the outside, we can see a crack in the rock just large enough for one person to squeak through, which then opens into a tiny grotto where Anthony spent his time. The physical tomb was an undeniable testimony of a world held in bondage to bodily death; yet it was also the spiritual symbol of a world held captive to the powers of sin, death, and Satan that were at work in the human soul. By taking up residence in a tomb, Anthony launched a dramatic assault on the power of the evil one, declaring the victory of Christ's resurrection over death and heralding the expectation of the second coming, where all sin and death will pass away.

In a similar way, the abandoned fort he later moved into provided a place to withdraw from the world's values and to reevaluate them in light of the Lord's own temptations in the desert (Matt. 4:1–11). Physical isolation encouraged spiritual detachment. The tomb and fortress thus became real places of spiritual warfare. They were also enacted parables of life as it was meant to be in the age to come.

Wondrous Is God in His Saints!

After years of desert living, some of Anthony's friends came and tore down the fortress door where he lived. The following is a description of what they saw:

> *Anthony came forth as though from some shrine, having been led into divine mysteries and inspired by God. This was the first time he appeared from the fortress for those who came out to him. And when*

they beheld him, they were amazed to see that his body had maintained its former condition, neither fat from lack of exercise, nor emaciated from fasting and combat with demons, but was just as they had known him prior to his withdrawal. The state of his soul was one of purity, for it was not constricted by grief, nor relaxed by pleasure, nor affected by either laughter or dejection.... He maintained utter equilibrium, like one guided by reason.... Through him the Lord healed many of those present who suffered bodily ailments; others he purged of demons, and to Anthony he gave grace in speech.[17]

This portrait of Anthony as a Spirit-filled man shows what a human being renewed in the image and likeness of God can become. His godliness stemmed directly from the grace of Christ. Anthony's victories over demons and his miraculous healings of the sick were not his own accomplishments but the wondrous works of Christ in his saint.

Athanasius could explain the physical and spiritual transformation of Anthony only in light of the conviction that Christ is the fully divine and coequal Son of the Father. Athanasius maintained with the Council of Nicea (AD 325) that the salvation and Christification of a mortal creature depended entirely on the power of the Son of God, who became human so that humans might become like God. One could only explain the great holiness of St. Anthony in light of this mystery.

PERSECUTION AGAINST CHRISTIANS WAS RAMPANT DURING THE EARLY CENTURIES. ANTHONY LEFT THE DESERT TO CONSOLE THOSE IMPRISONED IN ALEXANDRIA.

BRINGING JESUS TO THE DESERT

Again and again, his biographer takes pains to note that it was not Anthony, but *Christ* in Anthony, who gained victory over the powers of darkness. For the devil,

> who vaunted himself against flesh and blood, was turned back by a flesh-bearing man. Working with Anthony was the Lord, who bore flesh for us, and gave to the body the victory over the devil, so that each of those who truly struggle can say, It is "not I, but the grace of God which is in me."[8]

Anthony had such a transforming presence that just looking at him was enough to edify one's heart, as the following story illustrates:

A MONK PRUNES PLANTS IN THE GARDEN OF GETHSEMANE OF BIBLICAL FAME. ST. ANTHONY FILLED HIS TIME WITH GARDENING AND MAT-MAKING.

MONK AT ST. ANTHONY'S MONASTERY, ONE OF THE OLDEST IN THE WORLD.

CHAPTER TWO, ANTHONY OF EGYPT

Three Fathers used to go and visit blessed Anthony every year and two of them used to discuss their thoughts and the salvation of their souls with him, but the third always remained silent and did not ask him anything. After a long time, Abba Anthony said to him, "You often come here to see me, but you never ask me anything," and the other replied, "It is enough for me to see you, Father."[9]

Anthony Is "a Physician Given to Egypt by God"

In 311, a severe persecution against the Christians broke out in Alexandria. Anthony left the desert to minister to those who had been arrested and imprisoned in the city. Although he was willing to be martyred for Christ, he was spared and returned to the desert only to resume a daily martyrdom to his own will and fleshly pleasures.

Toward the end of his life he went even deeper into the desert and made an abode near a spring of water. He lived by gardening and mat-making. This "Inner Mountain" near the Red Sea (still called *Deir Mar Antonios*) would become his home until he died in 356. From there he continued to work miracles and counsel others, some of whom traveled great distances in search of an answer to their needs. Athanasius describes it this way:

It was as if he were a physician given to Egypt by God. For who went to him grieving and did not return rejoicing? Who went in lamentation over his dead, and did not immediately put aside his sorrow? Who vis-

SURGICAL INSTRUMENTS FROM THE ROMAN PERIOD. ST. ANTHONY WAS VIEWED AS A PHYSICIAN OF SOULS, GIVEN BY GOD.

ited while angered and was not changed to affection? What poor person met him in exhaustion who did not, after hearing and seeing him, despise wealth and console himself in his poverty? . . . And who came to him distressed in his thoughts and did not find his mind calmed?[20]

One day, God somehow revealed to Anthony that he was about to die. When his fellow monks heard it "they wept and embraced and kissed the old man. But he, like one sailing from a foreign city to his own, talked cheerfully and exhorted them not to lose heart . . . but to live as though dying daily. He told them 'Be zealous in protecting the soul from foul thoughts, as I said before, and compete with the saints.' "[21] When he had said this, the disciples embraced him; soon after, he died.

THE FAITH OF ST. ANTHONY THE GREAT

Though few of us are called to follow the monastic life, every Christian is called to imitate Jesus Christ, who displayed his presence in the life of Anthony. Among the many lessons we can learn from him, three are of special importance. Anthony teaches us the source, the means, and the goal of becoming like Jesus Christ.

A Transforming Presence to Others

The story of Anthony shows that God wants to transform us into the image and likeness of Jesus Christ. Anthony was convinced that the main obstacle to this goal was a sinful human heart. He knew that his inner nature was so out of sync with God's will that nothing but a strong dose of God's grace could cure him. That's why Athanasius declared the good news of the incarnation (God becoming human in Jesus Christ): "God became humanized so that humans might become divinized."[22]

The source of the spectacular transformation we see in the life of Anthony can only be explained in light of the incarnation of God in Christ. "The Word became flesh" (John 1:14) is the reality that made Anthony's "flesh become like the Word" to all who visited him. His very presence was enough to effect a change in the lives of others. Do you remember the visitor who testified, "It is enough for me to *see* you, Abba"?

That's the kind of wondrous presence God wants me to have too. Just as Anthony was "a physician given to Egypt by God," so I am to become a physician of souls to the people in my own circle of influence. When that happens, my very presence can become a powerful means of healing others, even if all they do is quietly abide in my company.

Transforming Our Spiritual Intelligence

One of the most important words among all the desert dwellers was the term *nous*. Sometimes *nous* simply means "mind." But often it refers to something much deeper than just intellectual activity. The term refers not so much to the rational nature of our thoughts and how we process information about the world around us such as science, math, or even God. Instead, the word *nous* describes an entirely different kind of intelligence. It refers to the central ability or function of our spiritual eyes. To put it simply, the *nous* is *the heart of our spiritual intelligence*. It is the central organ of spiritual perception. The closer we get to God, the more the Holy Spirit purifies the soul and enlightens the eyes of our spiritual understanding (*nous*).

Athanasius reported that Anthony "maintained utter equilibrium, like one guided by *reason*." Even on his deathbed Anthony admonished his fellow strugglers with these parting words about the *nous:* "Be zealous in protecting the soul from foul *thoughts*." For Anthony, and all the Fathers and Mothers of the desert, the *nous* becomes the main object of transformation. It's the thing that is in greatest need of change, and as it is changed, we are changed into the image of Christ.

All the activities of Anthony were aimed at transforming the sinful *nous* into the mind of Christ. That's why both God's grace and Anthony's effort are stressed in his biography. Grace is opposed to human merit before God, but it is not opposed to human effort. We can only become Christlike through the hard work of holiness. The aim is to heal the wayward passions of the *nous* by restoring them to their proper use through prayer, fasting, inner stillness, and other ascetical efforts. Anthony practiced long periods of silence so he could better hear the voice of God; he fasted severely in order to increase his hunger and thirst after righteousness; he lived alone so that when others came to him for help, he would be ready to counsel and cure them with a word from the Lord.

Transformational Love

Finally, as paradoxical as it may seem, the most famous hermit in all of Christian history teaches us an unexpected lesson. "He also said, 'Our life and our death is with our neighbor. If we gain our brother, we have gained God, but if we scandalize our brother, we have sinned against Christ."[23] For Anthony, the goal of Christlikeness was a perfected love for God and others.

Instinct suggests that this is not what we would expect to hear from a man who lived alone for decades in the desert. In our attempt to understand his significance, we must not see Anthony solely as an ascetic or a recluse, but as an intensely social being. His long periods of silence were often followed by a return to community life, where he healed and counseled others. Anthony's desert experience teaches us that ministering to others requires that we spend time in solitary prayer, nurturing our hearts and minds before God. We learn that solitude is deeply connected to our ability to love God and others well. Solitude should not lead to isolation but is the womb that gives birth to love.

Our patriarch of the desert, Anthony, modeled a transformed life that was based on the incarnation of the Word and a renewed mind that led to love for God and neighbor. Today his example invites us to join him in the desert. Once again, as Athanasius declared, "God became humanized so that humans might become divinized."

MOSAIC OF THE TRANSFIGURATION OF JESUS IN ST. CATHERINE'S MONASTERY. THE GOAL OF ANTHONY'S ASCETICISM WAS A "TRANSFIGURED" MIND (*NOUS*). THIS FEATURE OF HIS LIFE—COMMON TO THE ENTIRE MONASTIC TRADITION—WAS RELATED TO THE RENEWAL OF HUMANITY AS IMAGED FORTH IN THE TRANSFIGURATION.

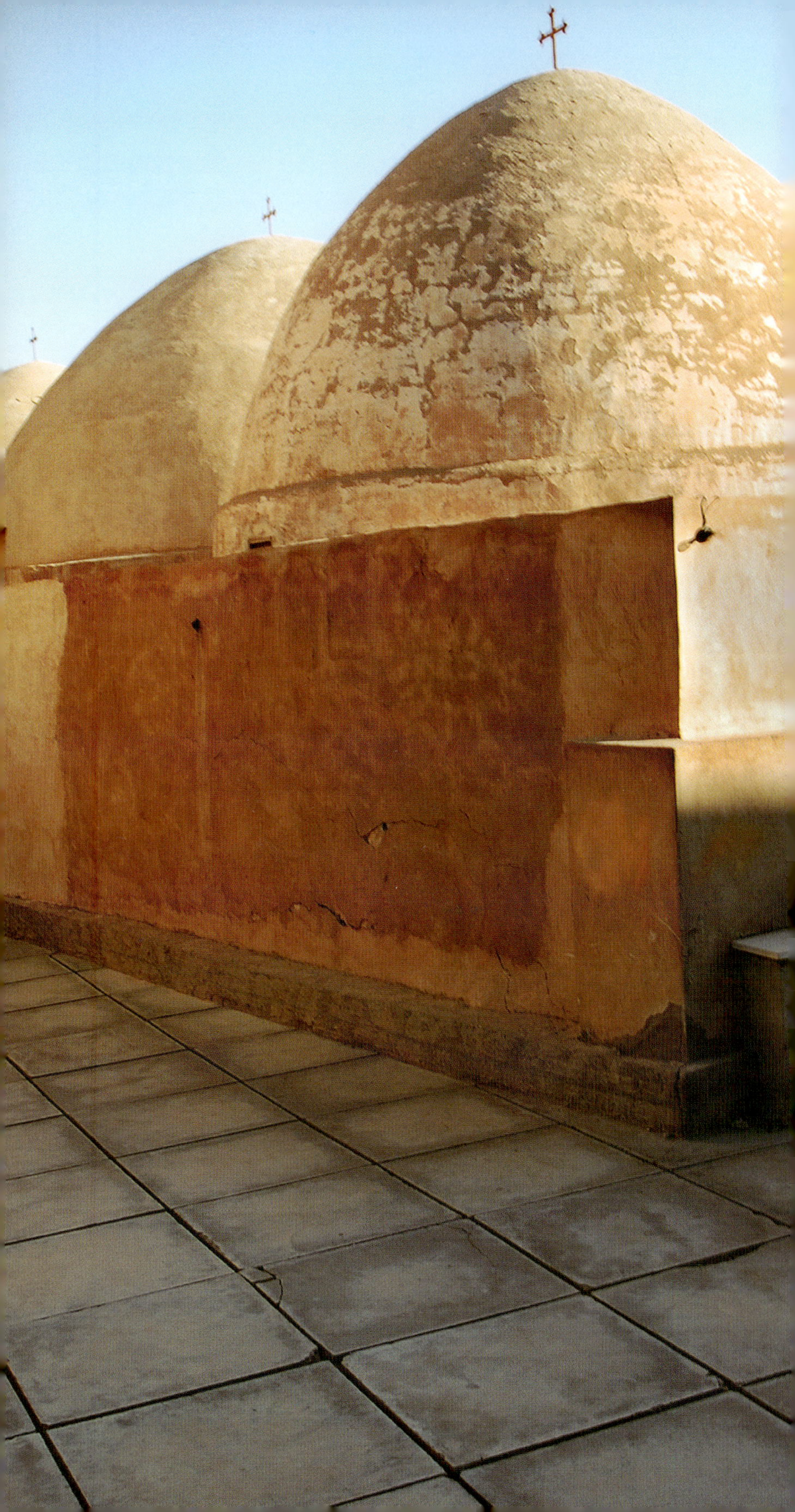

Chapter 3

Makarios of Egypt: Spirit-Bearer of Sketis

❦

ABOUT SEVENTY miles west of Cairo is a place called Sketis in the Valley of Nitre (*Wadi al-Natrun*). Father Ioan Bria, a Romanian Orthodox priest, had invited my wife and me to join him on a trip to the Monastery of St. Makarios at that location. The ancient historian Rufinus tells us that in his day, finding that place required one to make a perilous journey. There were no landmarks to lead the way. It was a vast wilderness that was accessible only if one followed "the signs and courses of the stars."

Rufinus's report was confirmed by our taxi ride. For miles, nothing could be seen but dry, hot sand and an occasional caravan of nomads. Then suddenly, out of nowhere, fortressed walls appeared on the horizon, resting on the desert like a ship at sea. It was the monastery of St. Makarios. We walked in and a monk warmly welcomed us: "Would you like some bread and water?" Father Ioan turned to us with a smile and whispered, "Do you see how *human* they are here?" The monk gave us a tour as he described a way of life that has reached as far back as the fourth century.

MONASTERY OF ST. MACARIOS
© Adam Reynolds/Corbis

A CIRCULAR WALL ENCLOSES THE MONASTERY OF ST. MACARIOS. THE LAND OF SKETIS (WADI AL-NATRUN) WAS THE TREASURE CHEST OF EGYPTIAN MONASTICISM. MANY OF THE GREATEST MONASTIC LEADERS LIVED HERE THROUGHOUT THE 4TH CENTURY. MANY OF THEIR STORIES AND SAYINGS ARE PRESERVED IN THE BOOK, "SAYINGS OF THE DESERT FATHERS."

St. Makarios of Egypt[24] (300–390) founded a monastic settlement in Sketis around 330. It became the birthplace of a golden age (fourth to sixth centuries AD) of some of the wisest

NOMADS WITH FIREWOOD LADEN CAMELS NEAR EL GOLEA, ALGERIA, NORTH AFRICA. THE AREA AROUND WADI AL-NATRUN IS A VAST WILDERNESS WITH ONLY THE OCCASIONAL CARAVAN OF NOMADS.

monastic leaders who ever lived. John Cassian, a contemporary who visited the area, tells us that "Makarios was the first of those dwelling in Skete."[25] In time, other spiritual elders (*abbas*) emerged from Sketis. They are unknown heroes to most of us living in the West, people such as Makarios of Alexandria, John the Little, Moses the Ethiopian, Paphnutius, Isidore, Arsenius, Poeman, and Serapion. We will meet some of them in chapter 6.

ST. MAKARIOS OF EGYPT

SKETIS: THE "HEART LAND" OF EGYPT

In the biblical world, names often reveal relationships. Isaac's name, for example, means "laughter" because Sarah laughed when she learned she would give Abraham a son in their old age (Gen. 18:10–15; 21–27). Later God tested Abraham by telling him to offer up Isaac as a sacrifice on a mountain in the land of Moriah. But God spared him, so Abraham offered up a ram instead and called the place *Jehovah-jireh*, "The Lord Will Provide" (Gen. 22:14).

The culture of the Middle East continued this biblical use of names. The name "Sketis" (pronounced SKEE-tees) described the experiences of the people who lived there. It means "to weigh the heart." It reflects an avenue of biblical culture in which the wilderness is seen as a place where God tests the heart. Just as God tested the children of Israel forty years in the desert (Deut. 8:2–5), and just as Jesus was tempted for forty days in the wilderness (Matt. 4:1–11), so this land "weighed the hearts" of the desert dwellers. Even this man's name, Makarios, is the New Testament Greek word for "blessed"—a spiritual quality he lived up to later in life (see the Beatitudes in Matt. 5:1–12).

ABRAHAM AND ISAAC BY MICHELANGELO MERISI DA CARAVAGGIO (1571-1610). SO ALSO SKETIS BECAME "THE PLACE WHERE GOD WEIGHS THE HEART" OF THE DESERT DWELLERS.

Stories and Sayings

By all accounts, Makarios was one of the most intriguing figures of Christian antiquity. Forty-one of his stories and sayings are preserved in the *Sayings of the Desert Fathers*. He was profoundly influenced by Anthony of Egypt, whom he visited twice during his life (AD 343 and 352). The details of his life, however, are so fragmentary that we cannot compose a complete biography.[26] The best we can do is to capture some of the most colorful snapshots of his life and comment on them, much like photos in a family album.

Makarios was born in AD 300 in the village of Jiber (modern Shabshir) in southern Egypt. Before becoming a Christian, he had a shady reputation as a camel driver and smuggler. We do not know the circumstances surrounding his conversion, but before the age of thirty he became a hermit and lived on the outskirts of town. When the villagers wanted to force him to be ordained, he fled to another village. After arriving, however, something awful happened to Makarios that would change the course of his life.

Flight to the Wilderness

Tragic events sometimes drive us to the wilderness. Just as Moses was driven into the desert after killing an Egyptian,

Makarios was driven to Sketis after he was falsely accused of sexual misconduct. The story is worth quoting in full, not only for its autobiographical content, but also for the humility and humor that kept Makarios sane through it all.

> Now it happened that a virgin in the village, under the weight of temptation, committed sin. When she became pregnant, they asked her who was to blame. She said, "The anchorite." Then they came to seize me, led me to the village and hung pots black with soot and various other things round my neck and led me through the village in all directions, beating me and saying, "This monk has defiled our virgin, catch him, catch him." And they beat me almost to death.
>
> Then one of the old men came and said, "What are you doing, how long will you go on beating this strange monk?" The man who served me was walking behind me, full of shame, for they covered him with insults too, saying, "Look at this anchorite, whom you stood up for; what has he done?"
>
> The girl's parents said, "Do not let him go till he has given a pledge that he will keep her." I spoke to my servant and he vouched for me. Going to my cell, I gave him all the baskets I had, saying, "Sell them, and give my wife something to eat." Then I said to myself, "Makarios, you have found yourself a wife; you must work a little more in order to keep her." So I worked night and day and sent my work to her.
>
> But when the time came for the wretch to give birth, she remained in labor many days without bringing forth, and they said to her, "What is the matter?" She said, "I know what it is, it is because I slandered the anchorite, and accused him unjustly; it is not he who is to blame, but such and such a young man."
>
> Then the man who served me came to me full of joy saying, "The virgin could not give birth until she had said, 'The anchorite had nothing to do with it, but I have lied about him.' The whole village wants to come here solemnly and do penance before you." But when I heard this, for fear people would disturb me, I got up and fled here to Sketis. That is the original reason why I came here.[27]

Makarios's response to the false charge is both humorous and humble. The subtle humor comes out in his private thoughts: "I said to myself, 'Makarios, you have found yourself a wife; you must work a little more in order to keep her.'" His shocking humility, however, would not let him deny the girl's false accusation! Instead, he trusted God for his vindication. When the truth of the matter was later discovered during childbirth, the real perpetrator of the deed was exposed and the villagers who abused Makarios sought penance and begged him to stay. But Makarios refused and fled to Sketis, where he could fulfill his calling in peace. Ironically, the false sexual allegation became the very catalyst God used to redirect the course of his life. Such were the humble origins of this famous monastic settlement. As the name implied, Sketis would indeed become a land where God "weighs the heart."

Desert Wisdom

Among the Desert Fathers, humility was the most elusive of all virtues—and the most powerful. That is because pride was the great enemy of the desert. Makarios understood that just as God drove the children of Israel into the desert "to humble and test" their obedience (Deut. 8:2), so also humility alone could conquer his pride and the destructive works of the devil within him. On one occasion he went to a marsh near his hut to harvest palm branches for his basket weaving. On the way back he encountered the devil with this thought-provoking inquiry.

> *When Abba Makarios was returning from the marsh to his cell one day carrying some palm-leaves, he met the devil on the road with a scythe. The devil struck at him as much as he pleased, but in vain, and he said to him, "What is your power, Makarios, that makes me powerless against you? All that you do, I do, too! You fast, so do I. You keep vigil, and I do not sleep at all. In one thing only do you beat me." Abba Makarios asked what that was. He said, "Your humility. Because of that I can do nothing against you!"*[28]

Humility was Makarios's strongest weapon against the destructive schemes of the devil. It rendered evil powerless while making the humble strong.

Another story is told that as Makarios was returning home from a desert journey one day, he caught a thief in the act of robbing his cell. As the thief loaded the goods on his animal, Makarios pitched in to help him. "He saw him off in great peace of soul [*hēsychia*], saying, 'We have brought nothing into this world, and we cannot take anything out of the world' (1 Tim. 6:7). 'The Lord gave and the Lord has taken away. Blessed be the name of the Lord' (Job 1:21)."[29]

In this account we can see how deeply detached Makarios

was from his earthly possessions. It reveals a profound level of inner tranquility and freedom from care. He held no animosity toward the robber. On the contrary, he was kind and compassionate toward him. Just as he had responded to the woman who falsely accused him of rape, so now his response to a thief is totally counterintuitive to our sense of personal justice. His detachment from material possessions and faith in God's care is all he needed to have "great peace of soul [hēsychia]." *Hēsychia* is a term frequently used in monastic literature to denote one of the aims of the Christian life, namely, "inner stillness" before God.

"The Jesus Prayer"

In volume 2 of this series, *Jesus, the Middle Eastern Storyteller*, we saw how simplicity was one of the hallmarks of Jesus' teaching methods. Makarios followed a similar pattern through his teaching on "pure" prayer. Pure prayer was the constant repetition of a short formula whose essential feature was the name "Lord" for God, as the following saying makes clear.

SCORE OF THE KYRIE ELEISON FROM THE 'MESSA A QUATTRO VOCI,' 18TH CENTURY. "LORD HAVE MERCY" IS A CONSTANT REFRAIN IN ALL LITURGICAL PRAYERS OF THE BYZANTINE ORTHODOX CHURCH. MAKARIOS HELPED POPULARIZE IT. THE NUCLEUS OF BYZANTINE CHANTS DERIVES ULTIMATELY FROM THE JEWISH SYNAGOGUE.

CHAPTER THREE, MAKARIOS OF EGYPT

Abba Makarios was asked, "How should one pray?" The old man said, "There is no need at all to make long discourses. It is enough to stretch out one's hands and say, 'Lord, as you will, and as you know, have mercy.' And if the conflict grows fiercer say, 'Lord, help!' He knows very well what we need and he shows us his mercy."[30]

Makarios popularized two short petitions that would eventually be widely used in Middle Eastern churches. The first, "Lord, have mercy" (*Kyrie eleison*), is constantly repeated in Eastern Orthodox liturgies to this day. A second petition is "The Jesus Prayer": "Lord Jesus Christ, Son of God, have mercy on me [a sinner]." Although the prayer may have been in existence before Makarios's time,[31] it is partly rooted in Jesus' parable of the Pharisee and the tax collector. There the repentant tax collector "beat his breast and said, 'God, have mercy on me, a sinner' " (Luke 18:13).

Several gestures in this parable shed light on the cultural continuity between the Desert Fathers and the biblical world of Jesus. For example, the tax collector's crossing of the arms in prayer was a dramatic gesture of humility still used in villages all across the Middle East from Egypt to Iraq. The beating of one's chest often points to sorrow or the heart as the source of evil desires (Matt. 15:19). Makarios's emphasis on simplicity in prayer reflects a cultural tradition that goes back to the very days of Jesus.

ST. JEROME IN THE DESERT BY SANO DI PIETRO (1406-81). BEATING OF ONE'S CHEST OFTEN POINTS TO SORROW.

The Rehearsing of Injuries

Life in the desert was a constant warfare against evil thoughts. Makarios, therefore, encouraged his disciples to fight against the mental temptations of remembering the wrongs that others had committed against them. He knew from experience that when one sat in the quiet desert for long hours, destructive memories enter the mind that lead to the rehearsing of old wounds. "Evil thoughts" (*logismoi*), as they were called, could attack the mind and distract one from contemplating the Lord. Discouragement and despondency could depress a monk plagued by such memories.

Makarios knew that memories could become powerful instruments for good or evil in the heart of a Christian. Just as Moses exhorted the children of Israel to keep the Passover as a remembrance of the Lord's deliverance from the bondage of the Egypt (Ex. 12:1–30), so Makarios urged his disciples to keep the remembrance of God constantly before their minds in the deserts of Sketis. For generations to come, Makarios was remembered for this famous saying: "If we keep remembering the wrongs which men have done to us, we destroy the power of the remembrance of God."[32]

Discernment

Makarios was renowned for his ability to read hearts and prescribe the proper spiritual medicine needed to cure them. His was the gift of discernment—an endowment often possessed by spiritual elders in these early monastic communities. It earned him the nickname "the Spirit-bearer."

Knowing how resistant we humans are to change, Makarios sometimes used subtle humor to sneak past the defenses of his disciples in order to impart a hilarious word of wisdom that would be forever implanted in their memory. The following story is one such example:

> *A brother came to see Abba Makarios the Egyptian, and said to him, "Abba, give me a word, that I may be saved." So the old man said, "Go to the cemetery and abuse the dead." The brother went there, abused them and threw stones at them.*
>
> *Then he returned and told the old man about it. The latter said to him, "Didn't they say anything to you?" He replied, "No." The old man said, "Go back tomorrow and praise them." So the brother went away and praised them, calling them, "Apostles, saints and righteous men."*

ARAB FAMILIES INCLUDE NOT JUST IMMEDIATE PARENTS, BROTHERS, AND SISTERS, BUT EXTENDED RELATIVES SUCH AS UNCLES, AUNTS, AND COUSINS. HERE THE FERRIS FAMILY CELEBRATES EASTER.

He returned to the old man and said to him, "I have complimented them." And the old man said to him, "You know how you insulted them and they did not reply, and how you praised them and they did not speak. So you, too, if you wish to be saved must do the same and become a dead man. Like the dead, take no account of either the scorn of men or their praises, and you can be saved."[33]

The story starts out with a familiar question found throughout the *Sayings of the Desert Fathers*: "Abba, give me a word (*rhēma*)." It was a request for a personal "word" from God that was specially tailored to meet the needs of one's heart. The elder then discerns the particular need of the inquirer and administers the remedy.

In the present story, Makarios spotted the trouble and demanded immediate action: "Go to the cemetery and abuse the dead ... [and] Go back tomorrow and praise them." The monk obeyed, went to the cemetery, and heaped insults and honors on the dead. He returned to Makarios, who then finally spoke the "word" he so desperately needed: "Like the dead, take no account of either the scorn of men or their praises, and you can be saved." The point? Be indifferent to the way the world measures our worth. Do not let your self-image or your inner peace be affected by either insults or accomplishments. Listen to God, not people.

There is a subtle cultural insight present in this story that most of us Westerners may miss but which a Middle Easterner would immediately detect. Family clans are deeply embedded in the cultural anthropology of the Middle East. Arab families include not just immediate parents, brothers, and sisters, but extended relatives such as uncles, aunts, and cousins. There is a much stronger solidarity there than in the Western world. Individuals within Arab families make decisions that are almost always guided by considerations of how acceptable those decisions would be to the entire group.

The young man in this story exemplifies the quandary that Middle Eastern relationships can create. We are not told exactly who was troubling the man—be they actual family members, brothers in the community, or someone else. But the cultural dynamics were clearly and strongly in play. The man felt enslaved to the opinions of others, and Makarios, knowing the culture firsthand, spotted it immediately. He saw what was keeping him from becoming the person God made him to be.

The power of this story comes from the way Makarios discerned the need and dramatized the lesson within the context of Middle Eastern culture. After all, who is going to forget making an embarrassing trip to the cemetery to shout insults and praises to the dead? The assignment was dramatic and unforgettable. That is because Middle Eastern teachers knew that lasting impressions were best created when a listener becomes part of the story they tell. Makarios, like Jesus, was a gifted Middle Eastern storyteller.

The Faith of St. Makarios

Unexpected Mercy

Makarios teaches us new perspectives on Christian living, some of which will deeply shock or challenge our cherished views. For example, Makarios's response to the young woman who falsely accused him of impregnating her is completely counterintuitive to our customary views of social justice. His humble acceptance of the allegation is appalling to us moderns, who are quick to settle the score with all perpetrators of injustice committed against ourselves, especially when they are of a sexual nature.[34]

In some ways, Makarios took the nonviolent approach of Martin Luther King Jr. and Mahatma Gandhi, who both refused the path of retaliation. Yet he did more than just passively resist the urge to retaliate. He actively used the false testimony of this woman as an occasion to grow in humility and faith. He deliberately forsook the security of satisfying his own needs for justice in the faith and hope that God would sustain him and, ultimately, reveal the truth of his integrity. In Makarios's hands, evil became a weapon of holiness.

Makarios also teaches us to watch for grace in the least likely places. The scandal of the false allegation became the occasion for God's guidance to a more fruitful life. Instead of staying in the same village, Makarios moved to Sketis, which in time became one of the most grace-filled lands in the entire world. He fulfilled his vocation with a posture of humility and submission before God's purposes and ways. When God asks us to accept a major change in our life situation for reasons

> ACCORDING TO MAKARIOS, EVIL THOUGHTS (*LOGISMOI*) WERE THE MAIN ENEMY OF THE HEART. MAKARIOS TAUGHT THAT REMEMBRANCE OF WRONGS WAS A TEMPTATION TO BE AVOIDED AT ALL COSTS: "IF WE KEEP REMEMBERING THE WRONGS WHICH MEN HAVE DONE TO US, WE DESTROY THE POWER OF THE REMEMBRANCE OF GOD." MARTIN LUTHER KING JR. AND MAKARIOS BOTH REFUSED THE PATH OF RETALIATION.

beyond our understanding, there may be a hidden gift of grace waiting for us.

Remembrance of Wrongs

Makarios teaches us another important lesson regarding the wrongs done to us by another. As noted above, he advocates in their place a constant remembrance of God: "If we keep remembering the wrongs which men have done to us, we destroy the power of the remembrance of God." To meditate on the wrongs of others is to create a major obstacle to prayer. Prayer should become the primary and constant activity of all that we do in life. Prayer is not something we *say* from time to time, but something we are to *be* all the time.

Evil thoughts (*logismoi*) are the main enemy of the heart. Makarios, therefore, suggests a practical strategy for defeating the evil thoughts that assailed the minds of his disciples, and us: "Meditate on the Gospel and the other Scriptures, and if a thought arises within you, never look at it but always look upwards, and the Lord will come at once to your help."[35] Such advice dealt realistically with evil memories without advocating their repression. When evil thoughts enter the mind, we are admonished not to

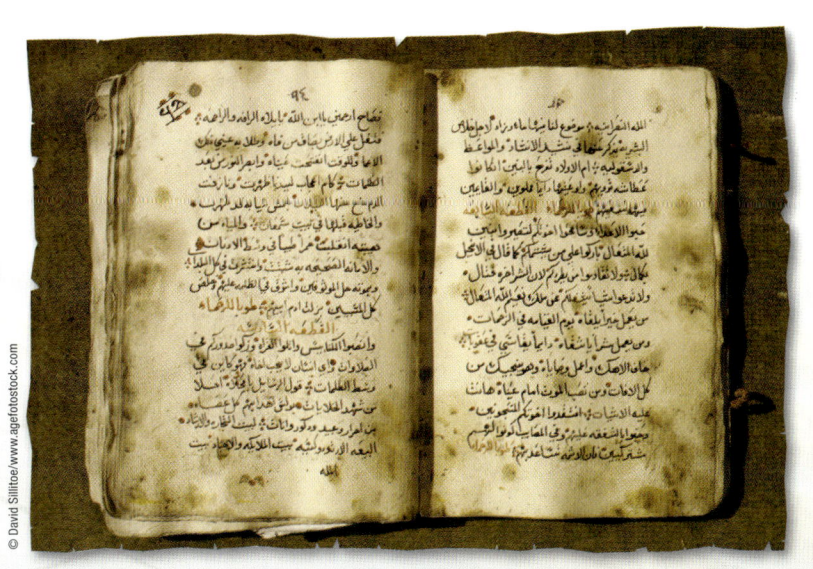

COPTIC BIBLE FROM THE MAHAREB MONASTERY, WESTBANK, EGYPT. SCRIPTURE MEMORY WAS AN IMPORTANT PART OF A MONK'S DAILY LIFE.

Rousanou monastery at Meteora in Greece. Monasteries in Greece have been influenced by St. Makarios. They often pray the Jesus Prayer: "Lord Jesus Christ, Son of God, have mercy on me."

"look at" them or deal with them in their own power, but to "look up" to the Lord for strength. Meditation on Scripture transforms the mind and creates new thought patterns. Scripture memory and meditation are the keys to victory over evil thoughts.

The Jesus Prayer

Makarios stresses the value of short prayers. Simple one-liners are a good way to communicate with God. The petitions "Lord, have mercy" or "The Jesus Prayer" ("Lord Jesus Christ, Son of God, have mercy on me"), which became widely used in later centuries, were partially developed by Makarios.

The Jesus Prayer even became the subject of a nineteenth-century Russian Orthodox classic titled *The Way of a Pilgrim*. The story is about an anonymous pilgrim who journeys across Russia in search of someone who could teach him how to fulfill Paul's command to "pray continually" (1 Thess. 5:17). Even though he was already a Christian, he knew nothing about The Jesus Prayer. So with only a pouch of dried bread crusts, and a pocket Bible, the pilgrim spent many months traveling throughout Russia visiting churches, monasteries, famous preachers, and bishops in hopes of finding someone—anyone!—who could explain the meaning of St. Paul's admonition. More than anything else, he earnestly desired to find a spiritual guide who could clearly explain how it's possible to pray without ceasing.

Finally, the pilgrim came across a wise old monk who was able to teach him the meaning of The Jesus Prayer and how to pray it "continually." The monk based his guidance on a book called the *Philokalia* (pronounced Fil-o-kal-EE-ah)—as noted in chapter 1, a collection of monastic writings that show, among other things, how to cultivate a rich interior life of constant "prayer of the heart." After learning The Jesus Prayer, the pilgrim joyfully declares, "I sensed within myself the greatest happiness from invoking the name of Jesus Christ, and I realized in my heart what he said: 'The kingdom of God is within you.'" From that time on, the pilgrim went about Russia zealously teaching The Jesus Prayer to whomever God sent him—the rich, the poor, the blind, and the learned. The final scenes portray the pilgrim with a professor, who became his traveling companion.

From this we learn the lesson of Makarios: Some prayers need only a single sentence to make a huge

THE ASSUMPTION CATHEDRAL IN THE HOLY TRINITY-ST. SERGIUS LAVRA - A FAMOUS MONASTERY IN RUSSIA. *THE WAY OF A PILGRIM* DESCRIBES A PILGRIM WHO JOURNEYS THROUGH RUSSIA IN SEARCH OF HOW TO "PRAY CONTINUALLY."

The desert tradition heavily influenced monastic life on Mt. Athos, the spiritual epicenter of Orthodox Christianity from c. AD 1000 to now.

difference in our lives and the lives of others. The Jesus Prayer or the simple petition "Lord, help!" enables us to "pray continually."

Few Christians have used small prayers for such great profit of soul as St. Makarios of Egypt. We, too, may find these prayers helpful, but they are not the only ones that have a powerful effect. We can make up our own. Our one-liners may be "Lord, form Christ in my child's heart," or "Lord, help me to keep my thoughts pure." Our best praying can be as simple as that.

We have seen that wilderness experiences are not for the faint of heart. As it was with the children of Israel, so the deserts of Sketis were a place of spiritual formation. It could make one either a great saint or a great sinner. History remembers

Makarios as a great saint. He died in 390 but his story lives on. It is the story of Christ in his saints. On January 19, Orthodox Churches still sing the following ancient hymn in his memory:

> *Dweller of the desert and angel in the body,*
> *you were shown to be a wonderworker, our God-bearing Father Makarios.*
> *You received heavenly gifts through fasting, vigil, and prayer:*
> *healing the sick and the souls of those drawn to you by faith.*
> *Glory to Him who gave you strength!*
> *Glory to Him who granted you a crown!*
> *Glory to Him who through you grants healing to all!*

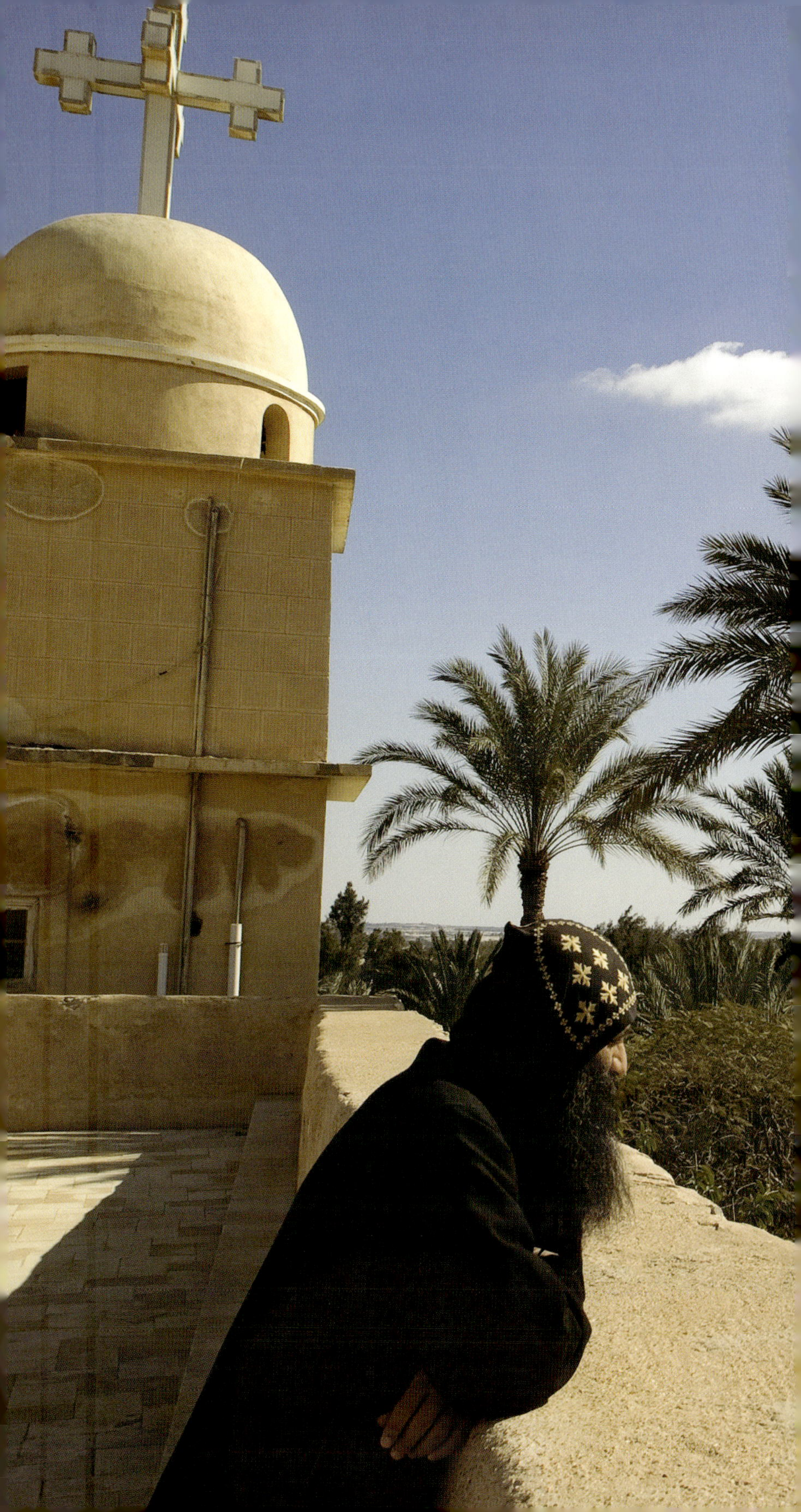

Chapter 4

Pachomius: Community Builder of the Desert

THE MONASTERY of St. Bishoi is one of the original monastic colonies of Sketis, the famous region we learned about in our previous chapter when we looked at St. Makarios. Father Ioan Bria from Romania invited my wife, Barbara, and me to visit St. Bishoi after we had seen the Monastery of St. Makarios. When we arrived there, a monk greeted us and escorted us on a personal tour. At one point he led us to a special room that contained valuable artifacts. It was like travelling back in time. Before our very eyes stood ancient stone cisterns, a large millstone, various oil lamps, garden tools, and other cultural objects used in the fourth century or earlier.

The more the monk described each artifact, the more my curiosity about him and his life intensified: "Tell me, what do you do all day?"

Monk looking out over the grounds at the Monastery of St. Bishoi.
© Mattes René/www.agefotostock.com

MONASTERY OF ST. BISHOI

"I pray all I can," he replied with an Arabic accent. "I go to church. And when I am in my cell, I read the Bible, pray for myself and my family, and say the prescribed prayers of the church. All of us here have been given a job to do. Some of us are bakers, some take care of the gardens, others clean the floors, and so forth. My job is to be a guide for visitors."

Ancient millstone, similar to those used at the Monastery of St. Bishoi.

"Do you follow any rules to organize your daily life?"

"Yes, we follow the *Rule* of St. Pachomius."

"St. Pachomius! You still follow his *Rule*? I'm astonished."

"Yes, we still follow the *Rule* that St. Pachomius gave us in the fourth century even until now. He told us what we must do to become more like Jesus Christ—to love God and our neighbor—so we follow his wisdom."

St. Pachomius mosaic, 12th century.

THE LIFE OF ST. PACHOMIUS

The simple conversation I had that day with one of Pachomius's modern disciples made a lasting impression on me. Now, as then, the quest to love as God loves is still the goal that guides the monks' every waking hour. From morning until night, the *Rule* of St. Pachomius continues to guide a 1,700-year-old community of desert dwellers. Their very land fulfilled the biblical prophecy when Joseph, Mary, and Jesus fled to Egypt to escape Herod the Great (Matt. 2:13–15), and then returned to Palestine: "Out of Egypt I called my son" (Hos. 11:1).

Community Builder

Tradition tells us that St. Mark, the gospel writer, founded the Egyptian church during the first century. Today, the Coptic (Egyptian) Orthodox Church is the heir apparent to this centuries-old community of Christians. The church is

A PRIEST EXAMINES A MONK'S CELL DATING FROM 4TH CENTURY, ST. ANTHONY'S MONASTERY.

still intimately tied to a monastic way of life that goes back to the early pioneers of the desert such as Anthony, Makarios, Pachomius, and others.

In our earlier chapter on St. Anthony, we learned that one type of monastic life was that of the hermit—someone who lives all alone in a cell, a cave, a hut, or a similar dwelling. Now we meet another form of monastic life known as communal or cenobitic (from a Greek term meaning "common life"). It is a type of life in which monks lived in a community or monastery led by a spiritual father (*abba*). The pioneer of this lifestyle was St. Pachomius, a younger contemporary of Anthony, though the two never met.

To say that Pachomius was the founder of a communal form of monasticism while Anthony was the first hermit, however, oversimplifies what we know of the movement. None of the original biographies about Pachomius or Anthony make this claim. There were Christians who lived solitary lives before Anthony just as there were communities of virgins before the days of Pachomius, even though their numbers were not high. Nonetheless, Pachomius was more successful and charismatic than other monastic leaders in the region, and that no doubt led to the rise of his popularity.

Conversion

Pachomius (c. 292–346) was born of reasonably well-off pagan parents south of Thebes (modern Luxor, Egypt) in the town of Latopolis. According to his biography, before he became a Christian, he was forced to join the Roman army at the age of twenty in a government recruitment drive during a time of war. He and other new recruits were locked in prison and "sunk in deep affliction," being tired, hungry, and fearful for their lives.

But something extraordinary happened one night. Local villagers came to the prison and gave food and drink to Pachomius and the other soldiers. Their kindness touched Pachomius so deeply that he asked, "Why are these people so good to us when they do not even know us?" His companions answered, "They are Christians, and Christians are merciful to everyone, including strangers."

The love Pachomius experienced that night made a profound impact on how he viewed Christianity in general, and monastic life in particular. After the war was over, Pachomius was discharged from military service without ever having to fight. He moved to the small village of Sheneset (Chenoboskion) in southern Egypt. Still, he could not forget the mercy that was shown to him by Christians while he was in prison.

MODERN TOWN OF ESNA (ANCIENT LATOPOLIS).

They felt his sorrows and afflictions as though they were their very own. By feeding the hungry, giving drink to the thirsty and visiting the outcasts in prison, these strangers proved themselves to be true sons and daughters of their heavenly Father (Matt. 25:36–40). Pachomius was so moved by their love that he believed in Christ and was baptized around 313. Love for God and love for neighbor would shape his vision of the Christian faith for the rest of his life.

BATTLE SCENE BETWEEN ROMAN SOLDIERS AND GERMANS, CA. 251/252 AD. PACHOMIUS JOINED THE ROMAN ARMY AT THE AGE OF TWENTY.

A Vision That Changed the World

Pachomius was a born community builder. After his conversion he devoted himself to the service of others in a variety of informal ways. His charismatic personality attracted others to look to him as a leader. After three years of service, he met a number of well-known monks and decided to become a hermit. One hermit in particular, Palamon, impressed him so much that in 317 Pachomius placed himself under his tutalage for the next seven years. Palamon taught Pachomius the spiritual disciplines that he himself had inherited from an older tradition: prayer, fasting, vigils, manual work, and almsgiving.

Pachomius was said to be gathering wood near the abandoned village of Tabennesi when he heard a voice calling him to do something that would require great faith. The voice said, "Pachomius, Pachomius, struggle, dwell in this place and build a monastery. For many will come to you to become monks with you, and they will profit their souls."[36] His spiritual father, Palamon, recognized the call as authentic, so in 323 Pachomius settled in Tabennesi.

While there, Pachomius reported a second encounter with the Lord one night through a dream. Three times an angel told him, "Pachomius, Pachomius, the Lord's will is for you to minister to the race of men and to unite them to himself." This new form of communal monasticism would be very different from the lifestyle of the hermits, but Pachomius did not perceive it as a negative judgment on the dangers of solitary life, just a different calling. His vocation was to unite the human race to God through prayer and humble service to others.

There is a parallel between the way God called Moses, Elijah, and Abraham and the way he called Pachomius. As it was in the biblical culture of the Old Testament, so Arab Christian culture believes that when God speaks to great leaders, he often does so through a voice or vision in the desert. Just as God called Abraham to cross the desert to go "to the land I will show you" (Gen. 12:1), so Pachomius was summoned by the Lord to build a monastery by faith in the deserts of Egypt. That is one reason why wilderness leaders were highly respected. Pachomius was a Christian hero who spoke from the desert with spiritual authority.

Like Abraham and other biblical leaders, Pachomius put his faith into action and soon things began to happen. Three Christians joined the community, then five, then fifty, then one hundred. Newcomers traveled through the wilderness to receive God's blessing in Tabennisi, much like the children of Israel who crossed the deserts to enter the promised land of Canaan. By the time he died, Pachomius had established a confederation of nine monasteries for men and two for women totaling over five thousand people.

Spiritual Father

Shepherd stories abound in the Bible. David called the Lord his shepherd (Ps. 23:1); kings of Israel were known as

A SHEPHERD WATERING HIS FLOCK OF SHEEP AND GOATS.

shepherds of the nation (2 Sam. 5:2; Ps. 78:70–72); and Jesus referred to himself as "the good shepherd" (John 10:11). Good shepherds care for their sheep by feeding, protecting, and leading them. The sheep follow because they recognize the shepherd's voice and trust it.

The same was true for Pachomius and his followers. His monasteries were composed of disciples who simply gathered around him, believing Pachomius to be a Spirit-filled shepherd. The chief shepherd of a monastery was called *abba* ("father," or "dear father"). It is a term of respect, intimacy, and endearment. (Our English word "abbot" comes from it, though without the relational qualities of the original language.) *Abba* comes from Aramaic, the language Jesus himself spoke. The apostle Paul used the word to describe the close relationship between God the Father and his children: "Because you are his sons, God sent the Spirit of his Son into our hearts, the Spirit who calls out, '*Abba*, Father' " (Gal. 4:6; cf. Rom. 8:15).

The ministry of a spiritual father or mother (*amma*) was not limited to the head shepherd of a monastery. More often, *abbas* and *ammas* were simple monks or laypeople to whom Christians went for spiritual counsel. It was the Christian community that recognized the gift of spiritual fatherhood or motherhood in a particular person. The initiative came not from the *abba* or *amma* themselves, but from their disciples who were in search of guidance.

Pachomius's monks pledged him their total obedience as the head *abba* of their monasteries. The authority of the *abba* came from his relationship with his flock. It was to be a relational authority of love rather than a dictatorial authority of rule. The emphasis on close relational ties between the *abba* and his disciples can be seen in the terminology Pachomius used when he spoke of his communities not as the monasteries per se, but as "the fellowship" or "communion" (from the Greek *koinônia*). He based it directly on Acts 2:42–47, where the believers "devoted themselves to the apostles' teaching and to fellowship, to the breaking of bread and to prayer." Following Acts 4:32, "all the believers were one in heart and mind. No one claimed that any of their possessions was their own, but they shared everything they had."

MODERN EGYPTIAN *ABBA*. ANCIENT MONKS PLEDGED PACHOMIUS THEIR TOTAL OBEDIENCE AS THE HEAD *ABBA* OF THEIR MONASTERIES.

Disciplines of the Desert

Virtually every major character of the Bible spent time in the wilderness:

- Abraham traveled through the desert on his way to Canaan.

SYRIAN DESERT—ABRAHAM TRAVELED THROUGH THE DESERT ON THE WAY TO CANAAN.

- Jacob fled from Esau and met God in the wilderness.
- Moses fled Egypt after killing a guard and encountered God on Mount Sinai, where he was called to be a leader of the children of Israel.
- David was a wilderness shepherd and then a wilderness fugitive before he became Israel's king.

ELIJAH FLED TO MOUNT SINAI AFTER KILLING THE PROPHETS OF BAAL AND THERE HEARD GOD'S "GENTLE WHISPER" (1 KINGS 19:12).

- Elijah fled to Mount Sinai after killing the prophets of Baal and there heard God's "gentle whisper" (1 Kings 19:12).
- John the Baptist prepared the way for the Messiah while preaching repentance in the wilderness.
- Jesus himself spent forty days being tempted in the wilderness.

Clearly, God uses the wilderness as a place for spiritual formation.

It is no wonder that Pachomius formed a Christian community in the Egyptian wilderness to reflect the biblical experience. He knew that he and his disciples could hear God better through observing silence; fasting and vigils could clear away the stony rubble from their hearts so that God's grace could be better received; and humble service to others was humble service to Christ. These and other spiritual disciplines of community life were spelled out by Pachomius, who composed the first known monastic *Rule*. The *Rule* was modified over the years to meet changing circumstances. But it was so influential that it provided a model for later monastic organizers, such as Basil of Caesarea in the East and Benedict in the West.

ICON OF ST. PACHOMIUS RECEIVING THE "RULE" FOR GOVERNING HIS MONASTIC COMMUNITIES.

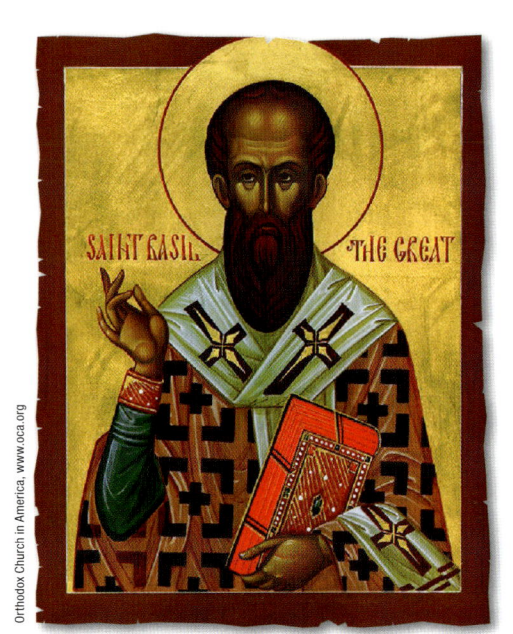

ANCIENT MONKS DISCUSSED THE STRENGTHS AND WEAKNESSES OF SOLITARY AND COMMUNAL LIFE. ST. BASIL FAVORED THE COMMUNAL FORM AS ILLUSTRATED IN THIS FAMOUS SAYING: "IF I LIVE ALONE, WHOSE FEET WILL I WASH?"

Outwardly, the *Rule* was a long, dry list of dos and don'ts for regulating the economic and spiritual life of his communities. It gave minute instructions for how the monks were to participate in commonly shared meals, and how they were to work and live together. It also instructed leaders in how to shepherd their monks, when to go to church, how to deal with troublemakers in the community, and other matters of daily life.

Early on, the rules were harshly applied by Pachomius. At one point his followers rebelled against him and were expelled. This was a failure that taught Pachomius an important lesson—that "to save souls you must bring them together." Rather than placing himself as the servant of others, future disciples would be asked to take responsibility for each other. The main intent of the *Rule* was to provide a rhythm of daily structure and direction for mutual growth in love for God and neighbor. At the heart of Pachomius's *Rule* was the explicit desire to create a community of biblically shaped disciples who were equal to each other in every way, socially and spiritually.[37]

Scripture and the Quest for Holiness

From Genesis to Revelation, the Bible is replete with God's commands to live holy lives. Joshua 1:8 summarizes scores of texts that speak of the centrality of Scripture for everyday life: "Keep this Book of the Law always on your lips; meditate on it day and night so that you may be careful to obey everything written in it. Then you will be prosperous and successful." That is why Scripture played a central role in the life of the Pachomian monasteries.

After joining the community, everyone was expected to learn large portions of the Scripture by heart. Pachomius himself set the example. He practically memorized the entire Bible and commented on it tirelessly to his disciples. Over 2,500 citations of Scripture appear in his *Rule* and in his daily pastoral exhortations to his community. Every person was required to memorize the book of Psalms and the entire New Testament. Even those who were illiterate were required to learn how to read so they could study and memorize Scripture. Pachomius insisted that "even if he does not want to, he shall be compelled to read."

Scripture memory was considered vital to a spiritually healthy life. The mental discipline that developed from the act of memorizing strengthened the observance of other monastic practices. Furthermore, there was an immense power in Scripture that assisted monks in their battle against the demons. It brought healing and encouragement by focusing their scattered thoughts on truth. The very words of Scripture were used

St. Gregory writing with scribes below, c.850-875. The illiterate were required by Pachomius to learn to read and memorize Scripture.

> The famous Gnostic Gospels were discovered in Nag Hammadi, Egypt in 1945. Their close proximity to the Pachomian monasteries has led some scholars to think they were originally buried by Pachomius's monks.

as weapons against foul thoughts that besieged their minds. Very simply, Scripture became the most important rule for the entire Pachomian community.

Early Christian worship was rooted in the liturgical practices of the Jewish synagogue, where the book of Psalms

> Old Ethiopian Christian Bible, written in Amharic on goatskin pages. The Bible is the Sword of the Spirit, which Pachomius told his followers they were to use as a weapon against foul thoughts.

Bringing Jesus to the Desert

figured prominently. Along with reading and memorizing Scripture, the brothers and sisters found the practice of reciting Scripture important in the daily services at church, especially the chanting of the Psalms. The monks' day always began at dawn with the recitation of Scripture as they walked to church. After arriving, one monk stood at the front and recited Bible passages, often Psalms. Constant exposure to the Word of God transformed their minds (Rom. 12:2).

A Lasting Legacy

Toward the end of his life, Pachomius seems to have recognized the extent of his influence when he reported:

> *In our generation in Egypt I see three important things that increase God's grace for the benefit of all who have understanding: the bishop Athanasius, the athlete of Christ contending for the faith unto death; the holy Abba Anthony, the perfect model of the anchoritic life; and this koinônia, which is a model for all those who wish to assemble souls in God, to assist them until they be made perfect.*[38]

The last days of Pachomius's life came when a plague swept through the region. Pachomius fell ill. As he was dying, he asked to be buried secretly in a nearby hill in order to keep others from making a shrine of him that would commercialize his body. He died on May 9, 346. Pachomius's memory is commemorated every May 15 in Orthodox Churches with the following portion of liturgical poetry:

> *With the streams of thy tears thou didst irrigate the barren desert, and with sighs from the depths of thy soul thou didst render thy labors fruitful a hundredfold. Thou wast a beacon for the whole world, radiating miracles. . . . Thou wast shown to be a radiant luminary to the ends of the earth, and didst populate the desert with multitudes of monastics, as with cities.*

The Faith of St. Pachomius

Community Life

The most obvious contribution Pachomius made to Christian spirituality was the creation of a communal form of monasticism. Yet, to speak of a community of monks is almost a contradiction in terms. By definition, the word "monk" means "to live alone." But in the Pachomian community, those who live "alone" now live alone "together" in the wilderness. Either way, whether alone as a hermit or alone together as a community, the goal of monastic life was one and the same: to love as God loves.[39]

Pachomius believed that spiritual growth best takes place within the nurturing context of a believing community. That is why everyone practiced Christian virtues together, obeyed a spiritual father, shared common goods, practiced chastity, and served one another through love. This way of life is almost totally opposite to how we think about Christian community today. For us, church is an optional activity, not a spiritual necessity; we value our gifts in general, but we do not specifically dedicate them to the building up of particular people in our local churches; we cherish independence, but not interdependence. Pachomius understood that to truly love God, we must actively love others, especially those who live and work nearest us. St. Basil the Great, a supporter of communal monasticism, said it best: "If I live alone, whose feet shall I wash?"

> Monks and nuns near Deir Mar Musa. Pachomius stressed living alone "together in the wilderness."

Spiritual Fatherhood

In modern times, evangelical Christians have rediscovered the ancient practice of spiritual direction. Spiritual direction is the help given by the prayerful presence of another person who helps us listen well to God. It can be a pastor as well as a friend or family member who is gifted with the ability to discern our needs and offer us a word of wisdom. Today entire Master degree programs are offered by seminaries in the art of spiritual direction.

But Christians of the Middle East have never forgotten this ancient practice. It is inherent in the very fabric of a spiritual culture that reaches back to the days of the great *abbas* and *ammas* of the desert. The early Christians realized that if we do not share our most intimate thoughts with at least one mature believer, we expose ourselves to the dangers of delusion and self-deception.

But to call them "spiritual directors" is misleading. The *abbas* and *ammas* didn't function as authoritative directors of the spiritual life of another. Rather, they were more like windows through which God's light could shine on the dark places of a disciple's life. Their goal was not to stand over others and direct their spiritual lives, but to become a window through which a disciple could see in the *abba* or *amma* the glorious realities of the Lord and thus become more conformed to his likeness.

In the Bible, titles are closely connected to everything that is intimate about the person. The third of the Ten Commandments told the Israelites not to take "the name of the LORD your God" in vain (Ex. 20:7). Jesus taught his disciples how to pray by addressing God as "Father" and to hallow his "name" (Matt. 6:9). In the world of the Middle East, people continue to grace their conversations with titles. Titles are powerful indicators of relationships.

The titles we use today toward our spiritual directors indicate how we regard spiritual authority. As I was growing up in a Lebanese-American home, we addressed our priests as *Abeena* or *Abouna* (depending on one's dialect), meaning "father." It is related to the biblical title *Abba*. We never addressed the pastor by using his first name or a nickname such as "Hey, Tony" or

AERIAL VIEW OF THE MOUNT OF THE BEATITUDES, WHERE JESUS TAUGHT HIS DISCIPLES TO PRAY. PRAYER WAS THE CENTRAL VOCATION OF ALL THE DESERT FATHERS AND MOTHERS.

"Hi, Nick." Whenever he entered the room, it was our custom to immediately stop talking, drop whatever we were doing, and literally stand up out of respect for the man and his office.

The Pachomian monks did something similar. They addressed their leader as *Abba*, which implied love and obedience.⁴⁰ Arabic culture has sustained this value inherent in biblical culture. It would be a precious gift if we in the West could recover the practice of spiritual direction and honor those who lead us, rather than secularizing them, as we often seem to do.

Spiritual Disciplines

Although the Pachomian *Rule* provided a pattern of spiritual disciplines that gave direction for growth in holiness, most of us reading this book are not monks living under it. We are people who live in a world of families and work. But two principles from the *Rule* can apply to everyone.

The first principle is to select one or more specific practices, such as meditation, fasting, or solitude, and do it regularly. Whether we are a full-time worker in the secular marketplace, a parent staying at home with children, an adult child now tending to aging parents, or a single person with few responsibilities, we will need to choose practices, in consultation with our spiritual director, that are realistic for us to commit to. These practices can be uniquely adapted to our specific personalities, circumstances, and needs.

The second principle we can apply from Pachomius's *Rule* is the grand goal of its design, namely, to produce love for God and neighbor through union with Christ in prayer. This goal is not restricted to those who live in monasteries or to those who encounter miraculous visions from God or are capable of heroic achievements of piety. The goal of love applies to all Christians at all times. Unless love remains the goal, our spiritual disciplines can become deadly ends in themselves.

Scripture Memory

One of the most important, lifelong lessons we can learn from Pachomius is that *the Scriptures are the single most important rule to guide our lives.* That is why he required all the brothers and sisters to memorize the book of Psalms and the entire New Testament. Sadly, Scripture memory is a lost art today. We go to seminars, listen to sermons, read self-help books, and attend Bible studies, but we do not make Scripture memory a central part of discipleship. In every course

ST. CATHERINE'S MONASTERY ON MT. SINAI. THEY ARE FAMOUS FOR THEIR BIBLICAL AND PATRISTIC MAUSCRIPTS, INCLUDING CODEX SINAITICUS.

OLDEST, BEST PRESERVED ICON OF JESUS AT ST. CATHERINE'S MONASTERY.

I teach, I make it a point to share with my students that I went through fifteen years of theological education for a Bachelor's degree, three Masters, and a PhD. But the single most important thing I have done in life is to memorize the Bible. Scripture is the soul of theology.

That is why, as parents, it is crucial to get the Scriptures into the hearts and minds of our children at an early age. It will protect them throughout life even if they do not comprehend all they are memorizing at the moment. Scripture memory is like writing a letter on a tender young heart that can be read, followed, and cherished with each passing year.

Pachomius's emphasis on Scripture memory followed a legacy inherent in the Bible itself. The Scriptures were Israel's manual for life in the wilderness. Pachomius knew that God delights in speaking his Word in the wilderness. In fact, according to the Scriptures, that is what the wilderness is for. God instructed the Israelites in the desert to bind his Word on their hearts (Deut. 6:4–9). When Satan (mis)used Scripture to tempt Jesus in the wilderness, Jesus responded by citing texts from Deuteronomy 6–10. Very likely, Jesus memorized the Scriptures from childhood as a result of the training of his

CHRISTIAN WORSHIPPERS PRAY DURING A EVANGELICAL RALLY IN JERUSALEM. MIDDLE EASTERN CHRISTIANS HAVE BEEN CALLED "THE FORGOTTEN FAITHFUL."

parents, Joseph and Mary. St. Paul admonished the Colossians to "let the word of Christ richly dwell within you" (Col. 3:16 NASB).

In time, the communal form of monasticism became popular and spread from Egypt to Sinai, Palestine, and Syria. To this day, these Middle Eastern communities have preserved and passed on a way of life that still echoes the desert disciplines of Moses, Elijah, and even Jesus. Perhaps that is one reason why Middle Eastern Christians have been called "the forgotten faithful." Their voices need to be heard today.

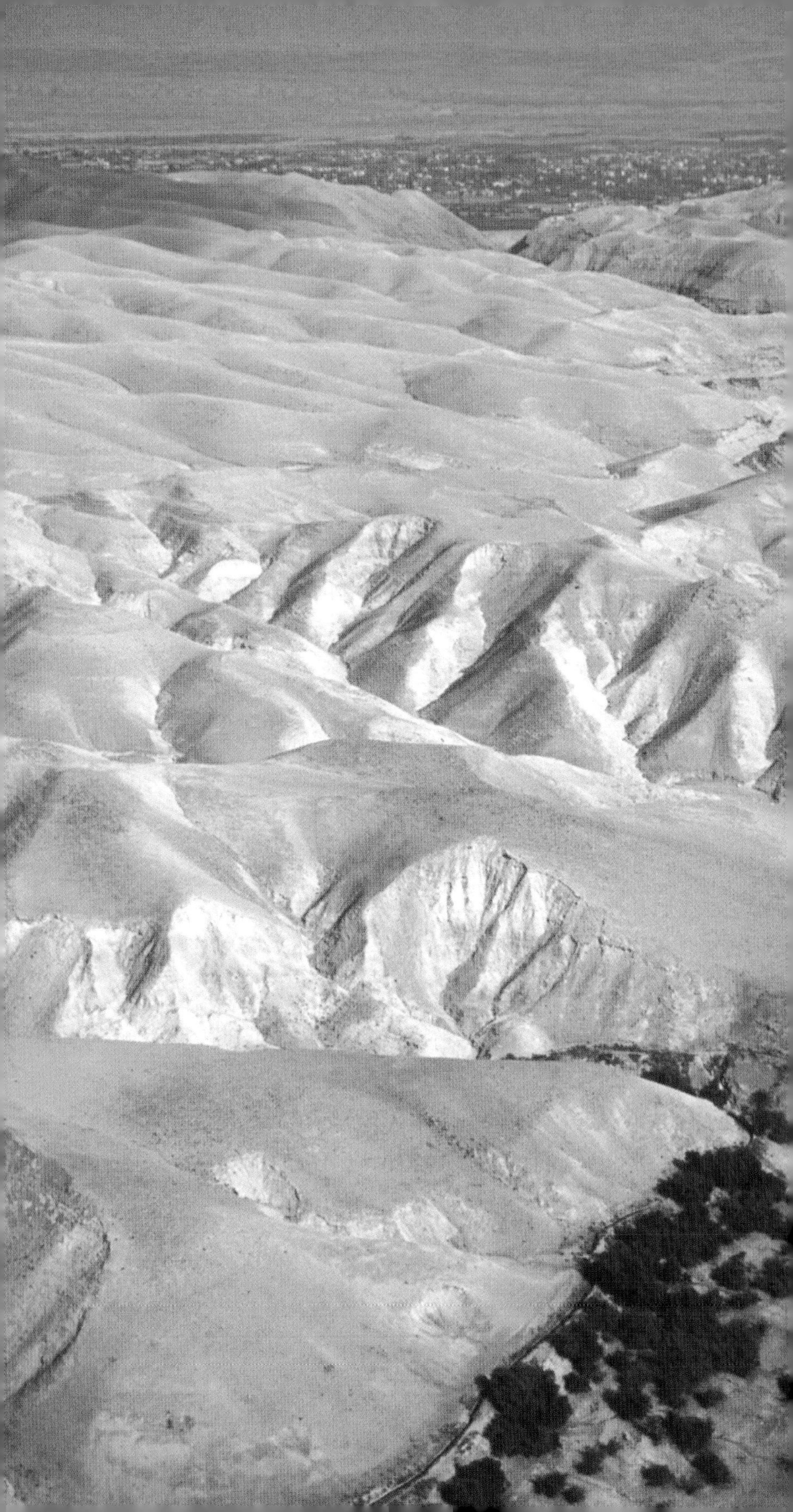

Chapter 5

MELANIA: MOTHER OF THE MOUNT OF OLIVES

LAST SUMMER my family had our largest reunion ever. Various relatives had always visited each other over the years but never like this. About sixty aunts, uncles, brothers, sisters, cousins, and kids traveled to Wichita, Kansas, from all across America to renew relationships and honor our grandparents, who had made it all possible nearly a hundred years ago. In the early 1900s my grandparents left their tiny villages in Lebanon, traveled one month by boat across the Atlantic, were processed at Ellis Island, and settled in Kansas to start a new life.

A highlight of the reunion occurred on the first night when we gathered at the large beautiful home of one of our cousins. Family photos taken across the years were displayed on the kitchen table. The picture that everyone's eyes went to first, that people picked up or lovingly touched, was that of our *Siti* (Arabic for grandmother), the great matriarch of the family clan. Each of us had fond memories of her and a mountain of heart-warming stories to tell.

Growing up with Middle Eastern grandparents, we all knew

AERIAL VIEW OF WILDERNESS WHERE MONKS HAVE LIVED.
© 1995 Phoenix Data Systems

that Arab culture was patriarchal. The man was the head of the home — well, in theory. If truth be told, *Siti* was the real power behind the throne. Despite her warm and winsome ways, she was proof positive that a strong woman in a patriarchal society wields as much power over a family as the man. Over the reunion weekend we swapped humorous stories and reminisced over how *Siti* would relentlessly call, coax, or otherwise manage to get something done. Our *Jiddi* (grandfather) was dearly loved, but *Siti* was the true director of the family.

SITI MARY FERRIG

The same can be said of St. Melania the Roman. She was not an Arab Christian, but the same dynamics were at work in her life. She was a strong female leader in a male-dominated society. She demonstrated that the pursuit of holiness was not limited to men. The monastic life was open to males and females as well as the rich, poor, educated, uneducated, slaves, and free.

It is true that men figure far more prominently in early Christian writings than do women. Accounts of the Desert Mothers are sparse. Only three women out of 131 elders found their way into the *Sayings of the Desert Fathers*: Sarah, Syncletica, and Theodora. Generally women ascetics did not live in the heart of the desert, but only on the outskirts near the Nile River or in the suburbs of Alexandria. To live alone in the great desert presented women with tremendous risks for their honor as well as their very lives.

It may well be, however, that there were many more women living a monastic life than what the literature suggests, though exact numbers are only guesswork. Their influence on the spiritual life of the church was no doubt great. In a book on the history of monks, the early church historian Palladius announced that he would report the feats of the Desert Fathers "as well as those of the venerable mothers who, with a virile force, led the battle for asceticism in a perfect way right to the end."[41] Yet there were no female creators of theology in the early church like an Athanasius, Basil, or Gregory of Nyssa. Few writings by Christian women survive from antiquity. We are left with precious little information about their lives, organizations, and beliefs.

Palladius uses a colorful description of female monks, namely, "the manly woman" — a phrase that conjures up visions of burly athletes. Some of the greatest "manly women" included Sts. Melania, Syncletica, Sarah, and Mary of Egypt. These women were ascetic trailblazers who overthrew their social stereotypes as inferior "weaklings." A story is told of *Amma* Sarah, who stood

ST. MARY OF EGYPT (4TH CENTURY), ONE OF FEW-KNOWN MOTHERS OF THE DESERT. SCHOLARS NOW BELIEVE SHE WAS A FICTITIOUS CHARACTER, BUT SHE REMAINS A MODEL OF REPENTANCE. SHE IS COMMEMORATED DURING GREAT LENT IN THE EASTERN AND ORIENTAL ORTHODOX CHURCHES. HERS IS THE STORY OF A GREAT PROSTITUTE WHO BECAME A GREAT SAINT.

CHAPTER FIVE, MELANIA

ST. MELANIA THE YOUNGER

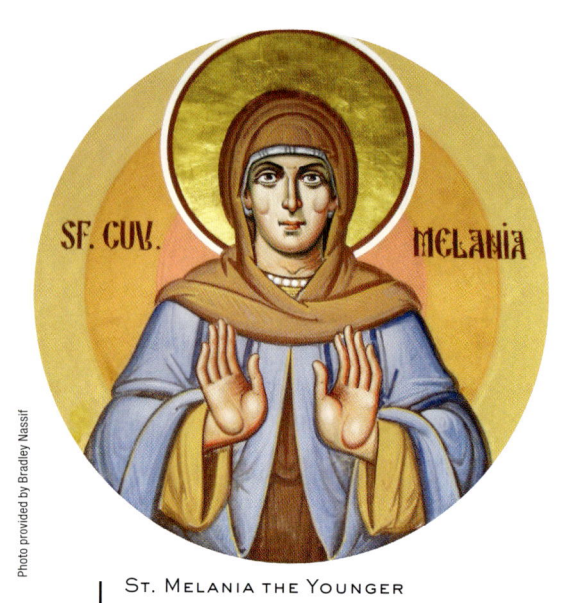

toe-to-toe with a group of Desert Fathers to remind them of her spiritual equality and superior stamina. When brothers from Sketis came to visit her, "*Amma* Sarah said to the brothers, 'It is I who am a man; and you are like women!'" Such "manly women" were not to be tampered with. Melania was one such person.

MELANIA THE YOUNGER (383/385 – 439)

The life of Melania the Younger has been cloaked in obscurity up to the present time. We often call her "Melanie," but her name in Greek is *Melania* (pronounced Mel-a-NEE-a) or sometimes spelled *Melane* (pronounced Mel-AH-nay). At times she is referred to as Melania the Roman since she originally came from Rome; others have confused her with her grandmother, Melania the Elder, since the two had the same name and did so much alike in their lifetimes. Much can be learned from Melania the Younger's modern biographer, Elizabeth Clark, whose translation of her "Life" we will use throughout this chapter by citing the paragraph numbers in parentheses.[42]

Although Melania is scarcely known today, she was famous in the early church. She was highly regarded by emperors and empresses and important church leaders throughout the Roman Empire, East and West, such as Augustine, Jerome, Cyril of Alexandria, and the Desert Fathers. Palladius describes her as a young woman with "such great virtue" that it "far surpasses that of old and zealous women."[43]

We can only pick a few flowers from the garden of Melania's

life as told by her friend and biographer, Gerontius. Gerontius was a priest who may have written the *Life of Melania* in 452/453 at the request of a bishop in Jerusalem, the heart of the Holy Land. The Mount of Olives was a special place just outside the walls of Jerusalem. It is significant because this was where Jesus taught his disciples about the end of the world (Matt. 24), where he prayed in the Garden of Gethsemane on the night he was betrayed, and from which he ascended into heaven after his resurrection (Acts 1:9–12). Apparently the bishop wanted to learn more about the local history of the Mount of Olives, and especially about the famous woman who had built on it two flourishing monasteries, a chapel, and a martyrion (a shrine erected over the grave of a martyr).

Days of Detachment

The story of Melania begins outside Palestine in the city of Rome. She was born to a wealthy family of the highest senatorial rank. She was a beautiful and intelligent woman, reared with a delicate upbringing. Her paternal grandmother, Melania the Elder, may have influenced her early in life. The grandmother had been extremely wealthy but gave away most of her possessions, dedicated herself to a life of virginity, went to Jerusalem to build a monastery, and devoted herself to learning

| MOUNT OF OLIVES

FORUM IN ROME, THE BIRTHPLACE OF MELANIA.

and to charitable causes. Her learning was legendary, especially for a woman in those days, so her granddaughter may well have followed in her footsteps.

From an early age Melania the Younger yearned to live a life of virginity and total dedication to Christ. At the age of fourteen, however, her parents forced her to marry Pinian, a seventeen-year-old son of a Roman, because they wanted grandchildren to inherit their wealth. The couple had two children, but unfortunately both died within a few years of their birth. Melania felt so depressed that she wanted to give up on life. Against their parents' wishes, she pled with her husband for them to live no longer as husband and wife, but as a spiritual brother and sister. This they did at the ages of twenty and twenty-four.

After Melania's father died, she inherited his wealth along with enormous properties located in Italy, Spain, Sicily, Africa, and parts of Western Europe. It has been estimated that her wealth was so great that it may have weakened the Roman economy when she later began to sell off her estates. Pinian's family wealth was likewise huge. His income swelled to 120,000 pieces of gold per year—a staggering amount when compared to a meager 8,000 pieces that could feed a fully populated monastery for an entire year. Together, Melania's and Pinian's combined assets made them an economic powerhouse. In today's terms, we would describe them as multimillionaires or possibly billionaires. They were the Bill Gates and Warren Buffet of the fourth century.

Despite their vast wealth, Melania and her husband did what every other great desert dweller did in those days. They detached themselves from all their earthly possessions. They heard the Savior's call to the rich young ruler as if he were speaking directly to them: "If you want to be perfect, go, sell your possessions and give to the poor, and you will have treasure in heaven. Then come, follow me" (Matt. 19:21). In 404 Melania and Pinian did just that. They rejected their pampered lifestyles and exchanged their luxurious clothing for cheap, simple ones. We can sense their joy, indeed their exhilaration, in her biographer's account of what happened next:

> They simply went around to all who were sick, visiting them in order to attend to them. They lodged strangers who were passing through and, cheering them with abundant supplies for their journey, sent them on their way. They lavishly assisted all the poor and needy. They went about to all the prisons, places of exile, and mines, setting free those who were held because of debt and providing them with money.... They purchased mon-

Roman gold coins with busts of the different emperors. Pinian's income was 120,000 pieces of gold per year! In today's currency, Pinian's and Melania's combined incomes made them multi-millionaires or possibly billionaires. They were the Bill Gates of the 4th century.

CHAPTER FIVE, MELANIA

asteries of monks and virgins and gave them as a gift to those who lived there, furnishing each place with a sufficient amount of gold. (par. 9)

This was just the beginning of Melania's charitable adventures. More came in the days ahead as she left Rome and traveled to Africa.

A Wise Giver and Bible Lover

Pinian, Melania, and her mother, Albina, fled from Italy in 410 just before the barbarian invasions and settled at Thagaste in North Africa, where they would live for the next seven years. There Melania and Pinian constructed two large monasteries and became friends with St. Augustine, one of the greatest thinkers in all of Christian history, who counseled them on how to distribute their money effectively. She became so skilled in her giving that "many of those who loved Christ furnished her with their money, since she was a faithful and wise steward" (par. 30).

It was during those years that Melania's learning and great love for the Bible came into focus:

She was a friend of learning. Indeed, she herself was so trained in Scriptural interpretation that the Bible never left her holy hands.... The blessed woman read the Old and New Testaments three or four times a year. She copied them herself and furnished copies to the saints by her own hands. (par. 21, 26)

STATUE OF WOMAN IN FINE CLOTHING, C.350 BC. MELANIA AND PINIAN TRADED IN THEIR LUXURIOUS CLOTHING FOR SIMPLE CLOTHES.

Following Paul's admonition to "train yourself to be godly" (1 Tim. 4:7), her daily disciplines included writing and the avid reading of Scripture, sermons, and the biographies of great saints:

She was by nature gifted as a writer and wrote without mistakes in notebooks. She decided for herself how much she ought to write every day, and how much she should read in the canonical books, how much in the collections of homilies. And after she was satisfied with this activity, she would go through the Lives of the fathers as if she were eating dessert. (par. 23)

St. Augustine by Sandro Botticelli (1445-1510). Melania met St. Augustine who counseled her on how to give away her vast fortune.

Patterning herself after Jesus in the desert, Melanie understood that "people do not live on bread alone, but on every word that comes from the mouth of God" (Matt. 4:4)

The Mount of Olives: Holy Ground for Holy Living

The time came for Melania and her small family to leave Africa and make their way to Palestine to the Mount of Olives. Melania regarded the Holy Land as a special place. In this series of books on Ancient Context, Ancient Faith, we have seen that from the beginning, Christians believed that the land where Jesus walked held promise for their own spiritual growth. Simply being there and seeing the places where Jesus lived and taught could inspire faith and bring spiritual renewal. When Melania entered the Holy Land, she was on a quest for intimacy with God that she believed could be deepened by placing herself in the land where God became human.

It was on the Mount of Olives that Melania practiced her most intense asceticism. She earnestly prayed, fasted, and worshiped. She had someone build her a little cell and there shut herself in for fourteen years, coming out only on Easter. She became extremely poor and dressed in the simplest of clothing. Melanie seldom counseled others and on rare occasion saw a few close relatives. At the end of that time, she founded two monasteries, one for men and the other for women, and a small martyrium to honor the relics of St. Stephen, the first known Christian martyr (Acts 7:54–60) and others. She lived in the women's monastery with ninety other virgins, whom she trained. Here are just a few of the spiritual teachings she imparted to her sisters in the Lord (par. 42–47, portions are paraphrased):

- It is necessary to be watchful and oppose evil thoughts.
- We are taught by the Holy Scriptures to guard our love for Christ and each other with all zeal. Without spiritual love all discipline and virtue is in vain.
- And since she feared that some of them might fall out of pride in excessive mortification, she said, "Of all the virtues, fasting is the least.... I leave fasting to everybody's own personal decision."
- Concerning love, humility, gentleness, and the other virtues she said, "A person does not blame either his stomach or any other part of his body, but it is inexcusable for any human being not to keep the Lord's commandments."
- The Devil is conquered by love and humility.
- The people who have born the outward garment of sanctity [her spiritual sisters] have made more serious trouble for me than the Enemy (Satan).... But I believe that the Enemy will not accuse me on the Day of Judgment of having gone to sleep holding a grievance against anyone.
- And before all else, let us guard the holy and orthodox faith without deviation, for this is the groundwork and the foundation of our whole life in the Lord.

This last saying reveals Melania's keen interest in Christian teaching. Just as Athanasius used *The Life of Anthony* to support the orthodox faith of Nicea concerning the full divinity of Christ, so Melania's biographer wished to present her as an example of sound doctrine whose "ardor for the orthodox faith" was "hotter than fire." He refers to her as a "good guide and divinely-inspired teacher," eager to converse "with holy and highly reputed bishops, especially those who stood out for their doctrine, so that she might spend the time of their conferences inquiring about the divine word" (par. 64, 36). When the Nestorian heresy arose (a teaching that separated Christ internally into two persons, one human and the other divine), Melania became a teacher of orthodoxy for both men and women:

> *Therefore many of the wives of senators and some of the men illustrious in learning came to our holy mother in order to investigate the orthodox faith with her. And she, who had the Holy Spirit indwelling, did not cease talking theology from dawn to dusk. She turned many who had been deceived to the orthodox faith and sustained others who doubted.* (par. 54)

Glories of a Noble Woman

Melania was widely known throughout the Roman Empire because of her family status, wealth, and godliness. Emperors, empresses, bishops, priests, and everyday people welcomed her with honors and great reverence whenever they came into her presence. "Holy men from every city and country (I mean the bishops and clergy) gave her glory and indescribable honor. When the God-loving

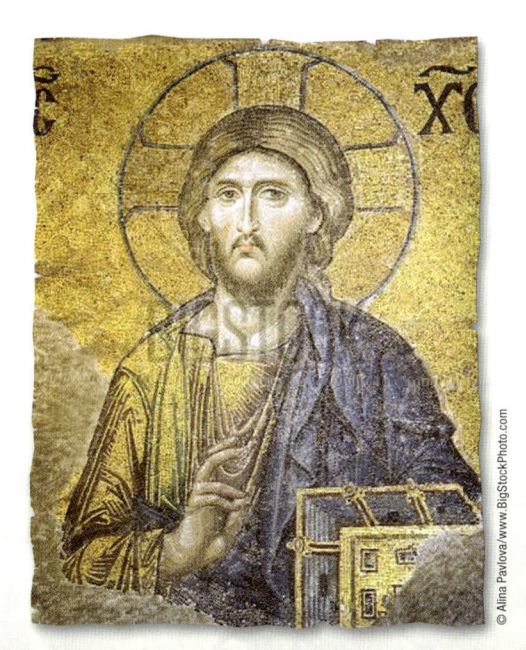

MOSAIC OF JESUS IN THE "CHURCH OF THE HOLY WISDOM" IN CONSTANTINOPLE. JESUS WAS FULLY HUMAN AND FULLY GOD, TWO NATURES IN ONE DIVINE PERSON, UNLIKE THE NESTORIAN HERESY CLAIMED.

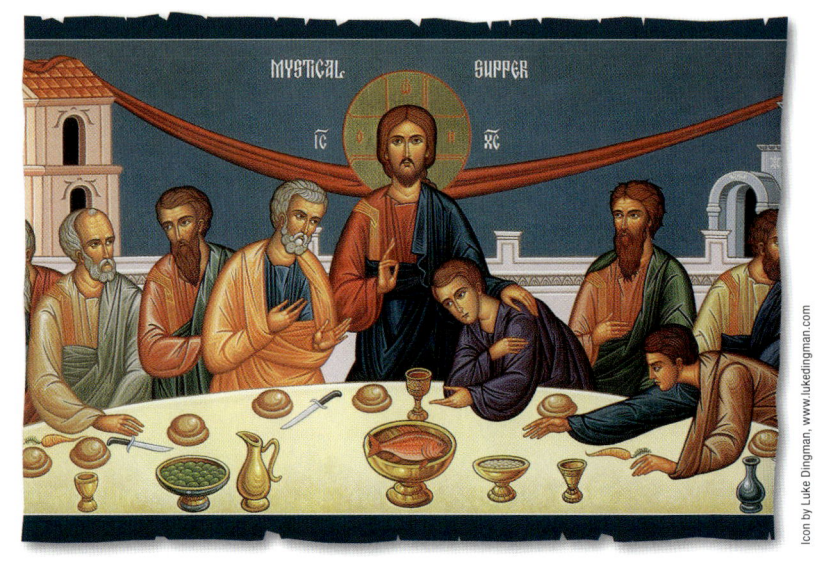

> Communion, here called "The Mystical Supper," was a central act of worship in the early church. Christians were content to celebrate the mystery rather than define it.

monks and pious virgins had seen her whose illustrious virtues they had heard about for a long time, they left her presence with many tears" (par. 67).

One reason why Melania acquired such profound godliness was because of her passionate worship of God. Over and over again, we hear of her constant devotion to the liturgical services of the church. In those days, monks and nuns regularly went to church throughout the day from early morning till late at night. But Melania deeply loved the liturgy, literally till her dying breath. On the Sunday on which she died, she asked to be placed inside the church close to the relics of the martyrs. She encouraged her priest to celebrate the liturgy even though she was "in total agony" from the disease she was suffering. As she was listening to the service, she noticed that the priest was so overwhelmed with grief that he could not pray loud enough for her to hear the prayer for the descent of the Holy Spirit on the communion elements, to which she called out, "Raise your voice so that I will hear the prayer (the *epiclesis*)."

That day, on December 31, 439, Melania took communion for the last time. Streams of clergymen, common Christians, desert dwellers, and devout monks from surrounding monasteries came to bid farewell to the renowned saint. We are told that Melania died just as she had always wanted: in the midst of holy people, gently, peaceably, joyfully, and on Sunday, the Lord's day, "in order that she might show in this her great love for the Lord and for his holy resurrection." It is no wonder that her biographer described her as "a truly noble woman" (par. 68). To this day, the Orthodox Church commemorates her life every December 31 with the following hymn:

> *In your fervent desire for the angelic life,*
> *You renounced the comforts of this earth.*
> *In watchfulness you practiced sobriety and deep humility.*
> *Therefore, most wise Melania, you became a pure vessel,*
> *Filled by the Holy Spirit, who adorned you with gifts,*
> *Attracting all to your divine fervor,*
> *Leading them to the Master and Savior of our souls.*

The Faith of St. Melania

Cheerful Charity

Melania was a model Christian philanthropist. A philanthropist is someone who gives time, money, goods, and efforts to help people in general, but especially the poor and needy. Melania was a major patron of monasteries and church buildings. She was a cheerful giver to anyone who was in need. She took vast sums of wealth and wisely distributed it in exchange for a life of voluntary poverty. No money, simple clothes, and little food became her way of life. She detached herself from material goods in order to develop a simple life in communion with God.

Melania's giving challenges us to readjust our relationship with earthly possessions. We recall Jesus' warning to the people of his day: "Watch out! Be on your guard against all kinds of greed; life does not consist in an abundance of possessions" (Luke 12:15). In Jesus' world, possessing land or wealth was closely related to gaining social prestige and honor. Melania, following Jesus, reminds us that possessions are not the measure of the truly good life. That is why she, a wealthy woman, gave it all away. Her cheerful charity reflects Christ's costly

VINEYARD IN GALILEE. IN JESUS' TIME, POSSESSING LAND WAS RELATED TO SOCIAL STATUS.

love: "though he was rich, yet for your sake he became poor, so that you through his poverty might become rich" (2 Cor. 8:9).

Theological Teacher

In previous volumes of this series, we have seen that every community of Christians throughout history has framed its understanding of theology within the context of its own culture. The same was true in Melania's day. The way ancient Christians understood theology was, in some measure, shaped by the cultural forces of a patriarchal society. Men such as Irenaeus, Origen, Basil the Great, and Gregory of Nazianzus were teachers of the faith. But St. Melania shows us that women could be great teachers of the faith as well. She exemplifies the power of a pious woman in a patriarchal society. Although she was not an ordained clergyperson or a creative theologian as these men were, she was still a teacher and defender of the orthodox faith. Both men and women came to her so that they might better understand Christian truth from a learned and trusted guide.

Melania's intelligence, love of learning, and comprehensive grasp of Holy Scripture argues strongly in support of women theologians. Today, there is every reason for us to follow Melania's example by encouraging women to pursue their gifts as spiritual guides and theological mentors. The early church blessed such women and was blessed by them. That double blessing is for us as well.

A Sacrifice of Praise

Melania understood the importance of disciplined worship in spiritual formation. The church's liturgies became the heart and soul of her life. She joyfully offered her worship, her sacrifice of praise to God (Heb. 13:15). Even as she was dying, her greatest longing was to be in communion with Christ through the bread and wine of the Lord's Supper. Central to her worldview was the New Testament teaching that sees the kingdom of God as both a present and future reality. She knew that intimacy with Christ was available here and now through communion with the living Lord.

The majority of Christian Arabs in the Middle East have continued to stress the centrality of worship in spiritual formation. Their liturgical calendars create a comprehensive cycle of worship that embraces the life of Christ and key moments in the history of the church. Their modern churches and monasteries have carried on a liturgical legacy across the centuries, whose very roots go back to the upper room, where Jesus "took bread, and when he had given thanks, he broke it and gave it to his disciples, saying, 'Take and eat; this is my body'" (Matt. 26:26). Melania was committed to the church's time-tested prayers. Her example beckons us to reevaluate our disconnection with historic practices of worship.

As we reflect on St. Melania and try to summarize her entire life in a few words, "heavenly minded" would seem to be an apt description. Her detachment from earthly possessions, her theological teachings, and her devotion to worship reveal a heart that was focused on a heavenly home. To Melania, her heavenly home was more real, and therefore more worthy of attention, than the physical world around her. Indeed, her whole life was an inspiring commentary on the admonition of St. Paul: "Set your minds on the things above, not on earthly things. For you died, and your life is now hidden with Christ in God" (Col. 3:2–3).

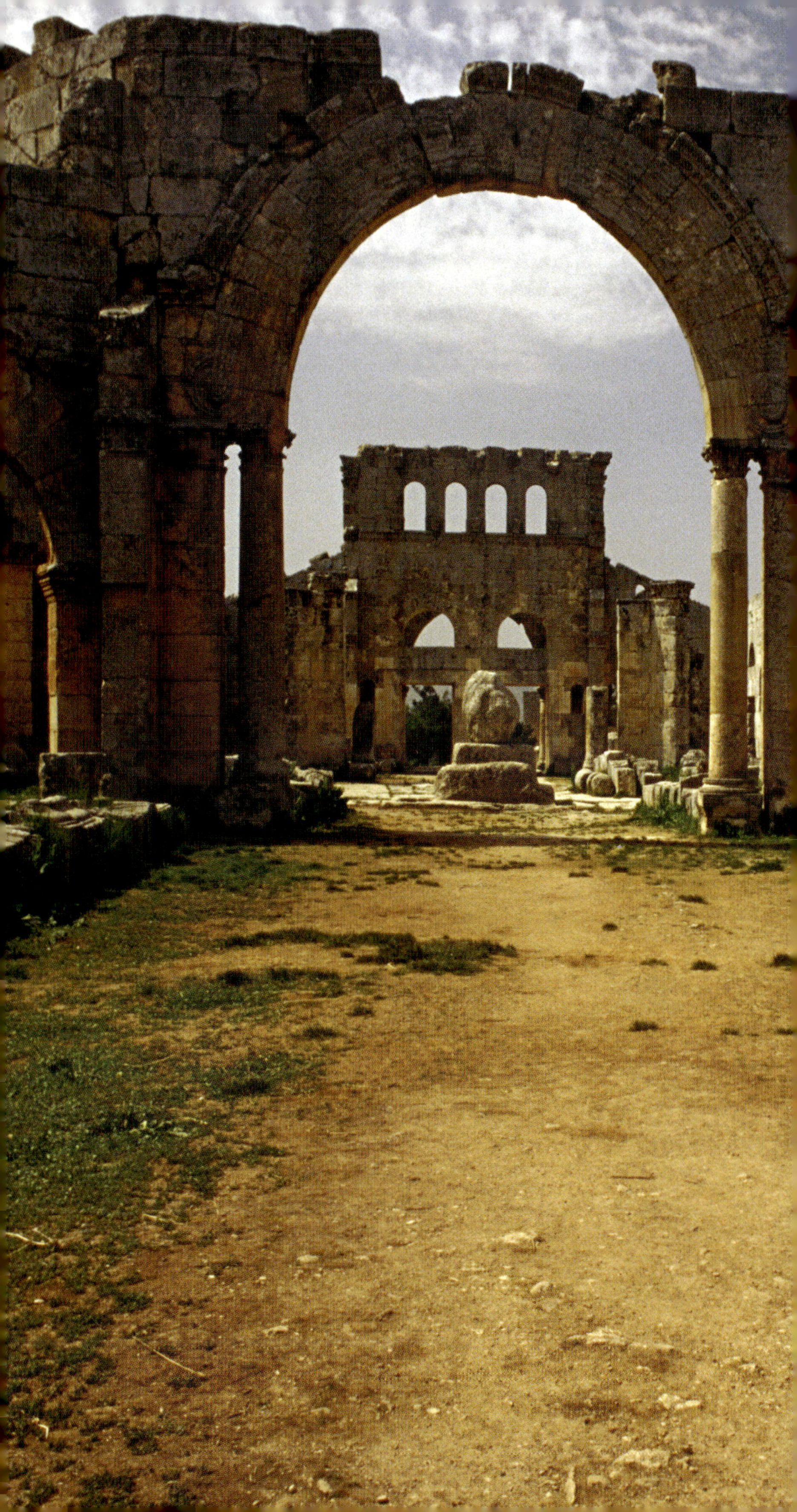

Chapter 6

Colorful Characters

❦

MIDDLE EASTERN families are close-knit. When I was growing up in Wichita, our grandparents, parents, brothers, sisters, and cousins all lived within ten minutes of each other. Every Sunday afternoon we gathered at Grandmother's house, entertained one another, told stories, worked, laughed, and cried together. We knew each other well.

One relative from the old country was Uncle Frank (*Mithqali Fud-lul-uh* in Arabic). He was unforgettable. His hard work, sense of humor, and witty ways became a recurring subject of conversation. He once told a story of his younger days in Lebanon in the early 1900s. Muslims had entered his village looking to kill him during a time of war. He was as good as dead had he not come up with a clever scheme to save his life. As he was being chased down the street, he ran into a relative's dry goods store, grabbed a dress off the shelf, threw it on, and painted his lips to disguise himself as a woman. The Muslim soldiers rushed into the store holding their machine guns in firing position. They looked right at him, cased the store, and quickly departed without incident.

Uncle Frank had outsmarted them. He died over fifteen years ago, but stories like this are alive in our memory. The

CHURCH OF ST. SIMEON
© Geoffrey Morgan/Alamy

mere mention of his name evokes warm hearts and smiling faces to this very day — that is, for those of us who knew him. Our children, however, never knew that uncle and seldom heard stories about him. He is one of the "forgotten greats" in our colorful history.

The same is true with our spiritual ancestry. As we end our story of the Desert Fathers and Mothers, there are many colorful characters we have yet to meet. Anthony, Pachomius, Makarios, and Melania are just a few of the illustrious leaders we have introduced from this forgotten family of Middle Eastern Christianity. In this, our last chapter, there are three other delightful people you may enjoy meeting in the family album: John the Little, Moses the Ethiopian, and Simeon the Stylite.

FRANK STEVENS

JOHN THE LITTLE (c. 339–409)

People of small stature can sometimes become great leaders. John was such an individual. He was one of the most memorable *abbas* in the Egyptian desert of Sketis, the spiritual treasure chest of the ancient world. He is called John the Little, John the Dwarf, or John Kolobos (from a Greek word meaning "small, stocky"). John's spiritual father, Ammoes, described him as "an angel and not a man." Paradoxically, his small stature was matched by a humility so compelling that "one of the Fathers said of him, 'Who is this John, who by his humility has all Sketis hanging from his little finger?' "⁴⁴

Abba John Learns the Value of Manual Labor

Although the details of John's life are incomplete, forty-seven of his stories and sayings are preserved for us in the *Sayings of the Desert Fathers*. Three stories are especially entertaining and challenging. The first occurs at the age of eighteen, when John went to Sketis. As a beginner in the desert, the path to loving God required that John come to terms with the conditions of his own humanity. A person could not expect to love God and others well until they had first embraced the harsh realities of life under the sun, literally. This meant that John needed to accept the daily drudgeries of manual labor as a normal way of life.

John, however, aspired to loftier things and wanted to be like the angels, who spend all their time praising God. He thought such a spiritual life could (and should) take the place of the menial tasks of everyday life. A humorous story describes his early idealism.

> *It was said of Abba John the Dwarf that one day he said to his elder brother, "I should like to be free of all care, like the angels, who do not work, but ceaselessly offer worship to God." So he took off his cloak and went away into the desert. After a week he came back to his brother. When he knocked on the door, he heard his brother say, before he opened it, "Who are you?" He said, "I am John, your brother." But he replied, "John has become an angel, and henceforth he is no*

ICON OF ST. JOHN THE LITTLE

CHAPTER SIX, COLORFUL CHARACTERS

longer among men." Then the other begged him saying, "It is I." However, his brother did not let him in, but left him there in distress until morning. Then, opening the door, he said to him, "You are a man and you must once again work in order to eat." Then John made a prostration [bow] before him, saying, "Forgive me."[45]

In time, John began to see physical labor as a tool for spiritual growth. He used manual work for soul work. One story describes how he integrated contemplation with weaving ropes and baskets. "It was said of him that one day he was weaving rope for two baskets, but he made it into one without noticing, until it had reached the wall, because his spirit was occupied in contemplation."[46] John came to understand that God uses everyday work as an instrument for purifying our passions and renewing human nature.

A Story about John's "Tree of Obedience"

When God brought Israel into the promised land, he performed a miracle by cutting off the waters of the Jordan River so the Israelites could cross on dry land. He then commanded the leaders of the twelve tribes to set up a memorial of twelve stones so future generations would remember the miracle (Josh. 4:5–7). These stones of remembrance provided a landmark with a purpose. God established a physical object that would remind them of his faithfulness for years to come. Arab Christians

CARPET DEPICTING FIGURES OF SAINTS, EGYPTIAN, COPTIC PERIOD, 4TH-12TH CENTURY. MONKS VIEWED WEAVING AND OTHER FORMS OF LABOR AS TOOLS TO SPIRITUAL FORMATION.

BRINGING JESUS TO THE DESERT

ACACIA TREE IN THE DESERT. JOHN THE DWARF'S LIFE WAS A LESSON IN OBEDIENCE. AFTER PUTTING A STICK IN THE GROUND AND WALKING 12 MILES A DAY TO WATER IT FOR THREE YEARS, IT GREW TO BECOME A HEALTHY TREE.

in fourth-century Egypt continued to use object lessons to teach spiritual truths as they preserved biblical culture. Perhaps the most famous is the one about John's "tree of obedience."

> It was said of Abba John the Dwarf that he withdrew and lived in the desert at Sketis with an old man of Thebes. His abba, taking a piece of dry wood, planted it and said to him, "Water it every day with a bottle of water, until it bears fruit." Now the water was so far away that he had to leave in the evening and return the following morning.

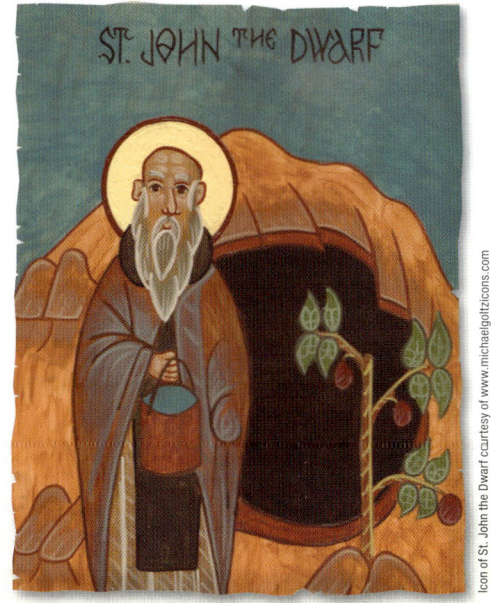

THE HUMILITY OF JOHN THE LITTLE HAD SUCH A POWERFUL INFLUENCE THAT IT WAS SAID HE HAD "ALL OF SKETIS HANGING BY HIS LITTLE FINGER." THIS ICON ILLUSTRATES THE STORY OF HOW HE WAS ONCE TOLD TO PLANT HIS WALKING STICK AND WATER IT EVERY DAY. AFTER THREE YEARS, SO IT WAS SAID, THE STICK BORE FRUIT. THE TREE SYMBOLIZES "THE FRUIT OF OBEDIENCE."

CHAPTER SIX, COLORFUL CHARACTERS

> *At the end of three years the wood came to life and bore fruit. Then the old man took some of the fruit and carried it to the church saying to the brethren, "Take and eat the fruit of obedience."*[47]

Today John the Little's "tree of obedience" is said to be in the deserted Monastery of St. John the Little in the Nitrian Desert. True, the tree one can see today is undoubtedly not as old as people claim, but that tree stands there as an enduring testimony to John's life of obedience. The story became so widely circulated in the Egyptian church that "obedience" became a prominent watchword among Egyptian Christians until this day. "Just obey" are common instructions that echo back to this "fruitful" story of John.

A Tender Story about a Prostitute's Repentance

According to the Gospels, prostitutes and adulterers were special objects of Jesus' love. An immoral woman washed the feet of Jesus with her tears and wiped them with her hair as she repented of her sinful ways (Luke 7:36–50); when a woman was caught in the act of adultery, Jesus saved her from being stoned to death while correcting and challenging her to turn from her evil deeds (John 8:2–11). In volume 3 of our series, these types of contacts between holy men and sinful women are shown to be socially disgraceful, yet the redemption in them is central to the mission of Jesus.[48] Early Christian writers continued to tell compassionate stories of Christ's love toward those fallen into sexual sins.

Our final story from the life of *Abba* John involves a similar outreach to a prostitute named Paesia (pronounced Pah-EE-see-ah). It is one of the tenderest stories in all desert literature. Paesia had been orphaned as a young girl. To make ends meet, she used her house as a small hotel. She was well-known among the monks at Sketis for her generous hospitality whenever they came to town. Over time, she spent her money and began to be in need. We are told that wicked men came to see her and persuaded her to become a prostitute. When the *abbas* at Sketis heard what had happened, they were deeply grieved and called on *Abba* John to come to her rescue. Because of his love for Paesia, John went to her home but made a surprisingly shameful request to the doorkeeper:

> "Tell your mistress I am here... and that I have something very helpful to her." ... Then Paesia got ready and said to the door-keeper, "Please bring him to me." As he was coming up she prepared for him and lay down on the bed. Abba John entered and sat down beside her. Looking into her eyes, he said to her, "What have you got against Jesus that you behave like this?" When she heard this she became completely rigid. Then Abba John bent his head and began to weep profusely. She asked him, "Abba, why are you crying?" He raised his head, then lowered it again, weeping, and said to her, "I see Satan playing in your face. How can I not weep?" Hearing this she said to him, "Abba, is it possible for me to repent?" He replied, "Yes." She said, "Take me wherever you wish." "Let us go," he said and she got up to go with him....
>
> When they reached the desert, the evening drew on. He, making a little pillow with the sand, and marking it with the sign of the cross, said to her, "Sleep here." Then, a little further on, he did the same for himself, said his prayers, and lay down. In the middle of the night, he woke up and saw a shining path reaching from heaven to Paesia, and he saw the angels of God taking away her soul. So he got up and went to touch her feet. When he saw that she was dead he threw himself face down on the ground, praying to God. Then he heard this: "One single hour of repentance has brought her more than the repentances of many who do not show such fervor of heart."⁴⁹

JESUS AND THE WOMAN CAUGHT IN ADULTERY (11TH CENTURY).

CHAPTER SIX, COLORFUL CHARACTERS

The meaning of the story is clear: the gates of paradise are opened wide through a humble heart of repentance. God will accept any sinner—even a prostitute—who comes to him at the last hour of life, if their repentance is as sincere and humble as Paesia's.

MOSES THE ETHIOPIAN (C. 332 – 407)

Slavery was commonly practiced in the biblical world. It was still going on in the days of *Abba* Moses, a slave who eventually became an elder in Sketis. Ancient records refer to him as Moses the Ethiopian or Moses the Black to distinguish him from others with the same name. He may not have actually been an Ethiopian since in those days calling someone an "Ethiopian by birth" was a common way of referring to anyone who lived south of the Sahara Desert.

We know little of his life before becoming a monk, but there are enough snippets of his past that point to a colorful career. Before coming to faith, he had been a slave of a government official, but because he was so disobedient and unmanageable his owner gave up on him and released him from bondage. He became a leader of thieves and cutthroats and began ravaging the countryside, robbing caravans and villages, and was rumored to have been a killer.

Then one day, something

MOSES THE ETHIOPIAN

ROMAN FRESCO OF SLAVE COMBING A GIRL'S HAIR (ITALY, 1ST CENTURY AD). MOSES THE ETHIOPIAN WAS A SLAVE WHO BECAME AN ELDER IN SKETIS.

changed Moses. Tradition, if true, tells us that he came upon a monastery in Sketis and intended to rob it. He broke into the *abba's* cell as he was praying and expected to see him cower in fear. But the holy man was unmoved by the sight of the towering figure who threatened to kill him. The *abba's* humility and peace of soul deeply touched the heart of Moses. He began to feel sorrow for his godless ways and abandoned his life of crime. He asked to become a monk and devoted the rest of his life to repentance and a life dedicated to overcoming the passions that had held such powerful sway over his soul.

Abba Moses' Teaching about Judging Others

As we saw in our chapter on Makarios, Middle Eastern storytellers often taught their disciples through enacted parables. A famous icon of Moses vividly portrays his character and an enacted lesson he gave on not judging others. It depicts him as a tall man with white hair, a physically strong build, and a facial expression of firm resolve. The icon is reminiscent of the time he was called upon by a council at Sketis to judge a monk who had committed an unnamed crime. Moses refused to come. Judging others was the one thing Moses avoided above all else.

A message was finally sent saying that everyone was waiting for him. Reluctantly, Moses went to the council, but he did so carrying a basket full of sand on his back. When he arrived, the basket was leaking, leaving a trail of sand behind him. He walked into the council saying, "I carry behind me my manifold sins where I cannot see them, and I come to judge my brother." His actions silenced the council, which promptly extended forgiveness to the brother.

Abba Moses' Teaching about Love and Rule-Keeping

Moses was also well-known for his hospitality. It was always a joy for him to welcome traveling brothers with open arms. A story records a dilemma he faced one day during Lent. What was more important: to fast in obedience to the rule, or to eat with the brothers and obey the law of love?

Once the order was given at Sketis, "Fast this week." Now it happened that some brothers came from Egypt to visit Abba Moses and he cooked something for them. Seeing some smoke, the neighbors said to the ministers, "Look, Moses has broken the commandment and has cooked something in his cell." The ministers said, "When he comes, we will speak to him ourselves." When the Saturday came, since they knew Abba Moses' remarkable way of life, the ministers said to him in front of

Monks during mealtime at the refectory in the Xenofontos monastery. Moses was well-known for his hospitality - sharing food and lodging with travelers.

> Shepherds were always searching for green pastures for their flocks.

everyone, "O *Abba* Moses, you did not keep the commandment of men, but it was so that you might keep the commandment of God."[50]

Moses knew God's love and that people were more important than rule-keeping, even good rules for fasting. He broke the commandment of humans so that he might keep the commandment of God. He never confused the means (fasting) with the end (love for God and neighbor).

Abba Moses' Teaching about Silence

In Bible times, shepherds moved from place to place in search of greener pastures. Some of them ended up dying in the wilderness for want of a better life. The same was true in *Abba* Moses' day when it came to spiritual matters. Men and women in the desert could live like nomads, but spiritually die by continually seeking "greener pastures" from the next (and next ... and next ...) *abba* or monastery.

It was in this context that *Abba* Moses provided perhaps the most frequently quoted saying in all monastic literature: "A brother came to Sketis to visit *Abba* Moses and asked him for a word. The old man said to him, 'Go, sit in your cell, and your cell will teach you everything.' "[51] The wisdom of *Abba* Moses was that the brother should not be jumping from place to place, always looking for new spiritual experiences. Rather, he was to

Syrian monasticism made its way to Russia when Prince Vladimir embraced Christianity in AD 988. St. Basil's Cathedral in Moscow takes its name from the holy fool St. Basil the Blessed (1486-1552). Basil once dared to warn Tsar Ivan the Terrible that his violent deeds would doom him to hell. During Lent, Basil mocked Ivan saying, "Why abstain from meat when you murder people?" Ivan feared Basil and refused to harm him.

stay put, sit still, and focus his attention on whatever it was that God currently wanted to teach him.

Simeon the Stylite (c. 390 – 459)

Radical Forms of Desert Discipleship

Historians of the day tell us about men and women in Syria and the surrounding region who engaged in outlandish spiritual practices that shocked and awed its observers, both then and now. Syrian monks fasted for twenty days in a row, wore iron shackles, slept on the bare ground, or stood motionless in prayer even in the midst of a howling rainstorm or heavy snowfall. Others lived like wild animals, eating grass or perching on rocks or in trees like birds; still others chained themselves to rocks, yoked their necks to heavy weights, bricked themselves up in caves, or imprisoned themselves in cages.

One of the most eccentric groups of these hermits was one called "holy fools" or "fools for Christ." These were Christians who pretended to be mentally deficient even as they prayed ceaselessly and meditated on the Bible. The Council of Gangra (389) eventually condemned some of their practices as unchristian, even though not all Syrians followed its decisions.

Simeon: The Greatest of Pillar Saints

Unlike other Syrians whose ascetical practices were condemned, Simeon is the best-known orthodox Christian from this tradition. Just as Zaccheus's fame came from his sitting in a tree (Luke 19:1–10), so Simeon's fame came from standing atop a fifty-foot pillar for thirty-six years in Syria. His pillar can still be seen in the middle of the courtyard of the Church of St. Simeon in the town of *Qal at Sim'an* (Arabic) near Aleppo, although it is

ST. SIMEON ON HIS PILLAR.

CHAPTER SIX, COLORFUL CHARACTERS

CHURCH OF ST. SIMEON

now only a five-foot high boulder because of centuries of relic-gathering by pilgrims.

Simeon the Stylite (from a Greek word meaning "column, pillar") was the first and most famous person in a class of holy men and women known as "pillar saints." Pillar saints were people who, in their fiery quest to please God and minister to others, lived on top of a column for years, praying, preaching, and practicing extreme forms of behavior. Their odd ways provoked observers to examine their own lives in light of the radical demands of the gospel.

A Countercultural Prophet

Apart from a little sleep, Simeon stood on top of his pillar all year round, even when one of his feet developed gangrene. A railing prevented his falling, and food and other necessities were brought on a ladder by his disciples. From there he prayed, preached the gospel, counseled, worked miracles, arbitrated disputes, stood up for the poor, and defended the orthodox faith. His prayers were so intense that every day he repeatedly bowed before the Lord in humble repentance. One bystander counted 1,244 bows (prostrations) in a single day, before he finally lost count! From the ground level, one could see Simeon perched high off the ground, arms raised in motionless prayer. During Christian festivals he often prayed in that motionless position from sundown to sunrise.

By standing on the pillar, Simeon visualized the angelic life as one who constantly praised the Lord. As a kind of mediator between heaven and earth, he offered prayers to God on behalf of humans and delivered heavenly blessings to those on earth. He was certain that his eccentric lifestyle was not of his own choosing but a special calling from the Holy Spirit. He frequently prayed, "Lord, grant me that on this stone, on which I stood at your command and order, I may complete the days of my life."

The people regarded Simeon as a saint—although a peculiar one, to be sure. Pilgrims came to him in throngs from all parts of the empire for wisdom and healing. During the heated debates that were raging in the Byzantine Empire over the full divinity and humanity of Christ, the emperor wrote Simeon to confirm the orthodoxy of the Chalcedonian Definition (451), which he heartily approved. Visitors came in throngs from as far away as Britain and Spain. There is even a remarkable account of how Bedouin tribes traveled from Arabia to Syria and were converted to Christ as a result of his pillar life and evangelistic preaching.

After years of the most amazing accomplishments and ascetic struggles, Simeon died atop his pillar. His strange life amazed and disquieted the entire

REMNANT OF ST. SIMEON'S PILLAR

CHAPTER SIX, COLORFUL CHARACTERS

Mediterranean world. Perhaps that is why his biographer, Theodoret of Cyrrhus, called him "the great wonder of the world."[52]

The Faith of Sts. John, Moses, and Simeon

Though little known, there are many lessons to be learned from the stories and sayings of John the Little, Moses the Ethopian, and Simeon the Stylite. Here are just four nuggets from their bags of desert wisdom we can use.

Your Workplace Is Your Monastery

Labor in the desert was not seen as a purely economic activity, as it is for us today, but as a tool for spiritual formation. John the Little saw a link between one's daily routines and personal wholeness. John and other Desert Fathers and Mothers believed that *our workplace is our monastery*. Wherever we are and whatever we do is holy ground. Our work is a place of redemption and a thing of beauty. It is where God meets us and transforms us. It is where our daily routines of cooking, cleaning, calculating, selling, building, doctoring, and everything else we do can shape us into the image of Jesus Christ.

CLERGY ARE OFTEN VIEWED HAS HAVING MORE "SPIRITUAL" JOBS, BUT IF WE ADD CHRISTLIKE PURPOSE TO OUR WORK, WE CAN CULTIVATE A VIRTUOUS LIFE. LIKE THE MONKS, NO MATTER WHAT WE DO, OUR WORKPLACE CAN BE OUR MONASTERY IF WE TRANSFORM OUR DAILY ROUTINES INTO A SPIRITUAL CAUSE.

Today, however, we not only separate sacred and secular tasks; we also tend to separate sacred and secular professions. We wrongly think that intimacy with God comes more fully to those who are free from secular toil. Clergy, missionaries, and Bible teachers are viewed as having "spiritual" jobs whereas caregivers, cubicle dwellers, salespeople, homemakers, truck drivers, and the rest of us have "secular" occupations.

To be sure, without spiritual purpose, work can make us despondent. Our routines can turn into cruel drudgery. But if we add Christlike purpose to our work, we can transform our daily routines into a spiritual cause. The salesperson will view their customer's problems as a spiritual opportunity to cultivate a servant's heart; a nurse's obedience to a doctor's request will become an exercise in meekness; writing "thank you" notes to former customers can create a deeper level of humility; correcting an error at work can foster the spiritual quality of repentance. If we contemplate the spiritual side of labor, we will come to understand that our work is not just a place where we till the soil; it is also where *the soil tills us*!

"Sit in Your Cell, and Your Cell Will Teach You Everything"

Some of us spend our day bustling about, constantly trying to make something in our lives nicer, easier, richer, or better. Yet the wisdom of *Abba* Moses suggests that we find time for stillness, away from our televisions, cell phones, instant messaging, and email activities, and take care to focus our attention on fixing what lies before us, and within us, as we listen to God. His wisdom suggests that we stay put and be content with our lives. We must not move from place to place or dwell on what we do not have—a new home, a new manager, better coworkers, or fewer problems. We are to learn how to deal with ourselves and our environment where we are, as we are—in our "cell"—because our problems usually lie within *us*, not within our circumstances. "Sit in your cell, and your cell will teach you everything."

Judging Others

Abba Moses insisted on refraining from judging others at all costs. This was especially true when people came to him for the express purpose of passing judgment on the actions of another human being. He once taught that "the monk must die to his neighbor and never judge him at all, in any way whatever.... To die to one's neighbor is this: To bear your own faults and not to pay attention to anyone else wondering whether they are good or bad."[53]

Moses could easily be interpreted to mean that we are to be morally neutral and to disregard evil entirely—that we should lose our ability to even "see" sin in others. Some of the Desert Fathers and Mothers actually adopted that perspective, and Moses may have been one of them. Nevertheless, Moses' virtual incapacity to see the faults of others was an expression of his freedom to love. By becoming free from the compulsion to judge others, he was better able to love God, show compassion to his neighbor, and foster silence, the goal of his monastic vocation.

In addition, because Moses was keenly aware of his own capacity for sin, his own struggle against the passions, he was loath to pass judgment on a brother. I wonder if our view of others' faults would change if we employed *Abba* Moses' advice. Would our inability to see those faults free us to love others more fully?

Holy Fools

If we were completely honest, many of us would admit that we have at least one relative whom we regard as highly unusual—perhaps even "crazy." Their eccentric ways set them apart from the crowd and make us feel uncomfortable. Their socks do not match, they sing off key, or they seem totally oblivious to what other people think or say about them. Yet when they open their mouths and speak, we notice something genuine and caring in their tone of voice. They are gentle and loving people, full of kindness and totally blind to the faults of others.

These "crazy" family members are not so different from Simeon's odd breed of "holy fools." Whether we like it or not, they are our family members regardless of their strange ways. Simeon the Stylite is one who startles and awakens us while, at the same time, challenging and humbling us to become authentic human beings. He shows us that the Christian life is not about escaping this world; rather, it is about countercultural engagement.

Like the prophets of old, Moses the Ethiopian reminds the church that the kingdom of God is not of this world. He insists that we cannot confuse the gospel's values with our culture's values. He exposes the underside of a form of religion that fuels our hunger for self-centered living and the easy assurance of an over-inculturated gospel. Perhaps most radically, he calls us to subvert the status quo at times in order to draw attention to the radical claims of the gospel. Do we need radical actions at times to draw attention to issues of poverty, abortion, and environmental responsibility? The good news of God's love can sometimes only be heard from the far margins of society.[54]

Parting Thoughts

IT'S TIME now to end our journey through the great deserts of Egypt, Palestine, and Syria. Together, you and I have traveled on the backs of imaginary camels to sit at the feet of some of the wisest people who have ever graced the earth: Anthony, Makarios, Pachomius, Melania, John the Little, Moses the Ethiopian, and Simeon the Stylite. We have time-traveled 1,700 years to an ancient civilization whose culture and spiritual life has a direct link back to the biblical world. That link still exists in churches and monasteries of the Middle East.

On our stops, we met just a few of the forgotten saints of the Middle East.

We observed how the physical landscapes of the desert matched the spiritual landscapes of their hearts. We saw these desert dwellers engage in the hard work of holiness and heard some of their most endearing and enduring insights on Christian living. Like Jesus, some of these Middle Easterners were master storytellers who dramatized their lessons through enacted parables or short, pithy sayings. Their wisdom has made a memorable impression that has not died. In varying degrees, their stories and sayings are still memorized, quoted, and lived within Arab Christian communities to this day.

For Middle Eastern believers, our brief survey of the great Desert Fathers and Mothers has not done justice to the liturgical, sacramental, and churchly realities that formed the context of their daily lives. For those underemphasized themes, I can only humbly ask for understanding. I was fully aware of these deficiencies as I sought to interpret this tradition for a largely Western readership, whose understanding of church life is far different from our own. To my Western readers who have now read this book, I would encourage you to visit an Arab Orthodox or Coptic (Egyptian) church to experience these Fathers' and Mothers' sense of spirituality and worship. Reading about their lives is one thing; experiencing their church life is another.

I hope you, the reader, have enjoyed keeping company with these delightful saints and profited from their wisdom. I hope they have inspired you to search out more of their stories and sayings than the few you have read in this little book. If you do, you will discover anew that the main point of their daily lives was to deepen love—God's Trinitarian love for us and our love for him and for each other. These desert dwellers are deserving of our attention because they reside in the company of those same biblical saints who "went about in sheepskins and goatskins, destitute, persecuted and mistreated—the world was not

St. George Antiochian Orthodox Church in Wichita, Kansas. The Antiochian Orthodox Church traces its origins to the apostolic age (Acts 11.26). American and Middle Easterners often worship together in America. Westerners are encouraged to visit a Middle Eastern church to experience the Mothers' and Fathers' liturgical life.

PARTING THOUGHTS

An interior view of St. George Orthodox Christian Cathedral. This community still celebrates an ancient liturgy. Western Christians are encouraged to visit a Middle Eastern chruch to better understand the liturgical context of the Desert Fathers and Mothers.

worthy of them. They wandered in deserts and mountains, and in caves and holes in the ground" (Heb. 11:37–38). Even though their wisdom was born in a world vastly removed from our own, these faith-filled heroes are astonishingly relevant to our modern world. Though they are dead, they still speak!

Our journey ends here, as we return to the edges of modern civilization. Upon dismounting our camels, we notice that a satchel we picked up along the way is no longer empty. It is chockfull of golden nuggets taken from the stories and sayings of the *abbas* and *ammas* of the desert. One nugget is Anthony's emphasis on Christlikeness through humility and transformation of the mind (*nous*) through the Spirit; others are Pachomius's Scripture memory in the community of faith, Makarios's simple "The Jesus Prayer," Melania's detachment from material possessions, John the Little's workplace as our monastery, Moses the Ethopian's refusal to judge others, and Simeon the Stylite's holy foolishness.

The satchel that holds them all together is our love for God and neighbor. This satchel of gold is not just for us to enjoy; it is given so that we might enrich those around us. Our modern world longs for this simple wisdom—the wisdom of holy people in a holy land that stretches back to the days of the Bible.

NOTES

1. Philip Jenkins, *The Lost History of Christianity* (New York: HarperOne, 2008), 6.
2. Bradley Nassif, "The Poverty of Love," *Christianity Today* 52/5 (May 2008): 34–37; see www.ctlibrary.com/ct/2008/may/11.34.html.
3. See *Patrologia Graeca* (compiled by J. P. Migne; Paris, 1857–1887), 25:192.
4. Darrell Johnson, *Experiencing the Trinity* (Vancouver: Regent College Press, 1998), 62.
5. *The Life of Anthony and Letter to Marcellinus* (trans. Robert Gregg; New York: Paulist, 1980).
6. *Sayings of the Desert Fathers* (trans. Benedicta Ward; Kalamazoo, MI: Cistercian Publications, 1975). Note also its companion volume: *The Desert Fathers: Sayings of Early Christian Monks* (trans. Benedicta Ward; New York: Penguin, 2003), which is arranged by topic. The best introduction to the teachings of the Desert Fathers and Mothers is Roberta Bondi, *To Love as God Loves* (New York: Fortress, 1983). For daily devotions see *Daily Readings with the Desert Fathers* (ed. Benedicta Ward; New York: Templegate, 1988).
7. My paraphrase of *The Life of Antony* (trans. R.C. Gregg; New York: Paulist, 1980), 98–99. Athanasius was a bishop and strong defender of the divinity of Christ and the Nicene Creed in the fourth century.
8. Augustine, *Confessions* 8.6.
9. *The Philokalia* is a five-volume work compiled by two monks on Mount Athos in Greece in the eighteenth century (see the English version, *The Philokalia* [trans. G. E. H. Palmer, Philip Sherrard, and Kallistos Ware; London: Faber & Faber, 1986–]; four vols. are out, and a fifth volume is forthcoming). A collection of essays is in *The Philokalia: Exploring a Classic Text of Orthodox Spirituality* (eds. Brock Bingaman and Bradley Nassif; New York: Oxford Univ. Press, 2012).
10. Quotation paraphrased from *Book of Prayers and Services*, compiled by Seraphim Nassar (Englewood, NY: Antiochian Orthodox Archdiocese of North America, 1979), 485.
11. Called deification or *theôsis;* see chapter 1, pp. 31–32.
12. *Life of Anthony*, 32.
13. Ibid., 33.
14. Ibid., 42.

15. *Sayings of the Desert Fathers* (trans. Benedicta Ward; Kalamazoo, MI: Cistercian Publications, 1975); "Anthony," #7 (p. 3).
16. Gary Burge, *The Bible and the Land* (Grand Rapids: Zondervan, 2008), esp. 37–48.
17. *Life of Anthony*, 42.
18. Ibid., 34 quoting 1 Cor. 15:10.
19. *Sayings of the Desert Fathers*, "Anthony," #27 (p. 7, emphasis mine).
20. *The Life of Anthony*, 94.
21. Ibid., 95.
22. Athanasius, *On the Incarnation of the Word* (foreword by C. S. Lewis; Yonkers, NY: St. Vladimir's Seminary Press, 1976), paragraph 54. Although Athanasius doesn't use the Greek term *theôsis* here, he uses the sister word *theopoiçsis*, which means roughly "divinization."
23. *Sayings of the Desert Fathers*, "Anthony," #9 (p. 3).
24. He is also known as Makarios the Great. Ancient and modern commentators sometimes confuse him with his contemporary Makarios the Alexandrian or a later Syrian monk whom scholars refer to as Pseudo-Makarios, whose "prayer of the heart" became very influential in the Eastern Orthodox tradition.
25. John Cassian, *Conferences* (trans. Colm Luibheid; New York: Paulist, 1985), 176.
26. The best recent source is a translation and introduction by Tim Vivian, *Saint Macarius the Spiritbearer: Coptic Texts Relating to Saint Macarius the Great* (Yonkers, NY: St. Vladimir's Press, 2004).
27. *Sayings of the Desert Fathers* (trans. Benedicta Ward; Kalamazoo, MI: Cistercian Publications, 1975); "Makarios," #1 (pp. 124–25).
28. Ibid., #11 (pp. 129–30).
29. Ibid., #18 (p. 131).
30. Ibid., #19 (p. 131).
31. See John Meyendorff, *St. Gregory Palamas and Orthodox Spirituality* (Yonkers, NY: St. Vladimir's Seminary Press, 1974), 24–29.
32. *Sayings of the Desert Fathers*, "Makarios," #36 (p. 136).
33. Ibid., #23, p. 132.
34. An alternate reading of Markarios's response to the young girl's accusation is found in a much later account of the story written over two hundred years after the account given in the alphabetical collection of *Sayings of the Desert Fathers*. In that later rendition, the young man who impregnated the woman was her cousin and fiancé. The couple allowed themselves to get too close to each other and eventually lost their virginity. After Makarios was blamed and badly beaten, he denies the girl's charge saying to the boy's father, "What an injustice! I do not acknowledge this charge brought against me!" (Vivian, *Saint Macarius the Spiritbearer*, 166). We will probably never know for certain whether this account or the one in the alphabetical collection is authentic, but his silent acceptance of the wrong rather than his objection to the injustice fits best with his known character and the earlier text that originally recorded the incident.
35. *Sayings of the Desert Fathers*, "Makarios," #3 (p. 127). Other monks utilized different strategies for dealing with evil thoughts. See "On Watchfulness and Holiness" by St. Hesychius the Priest, in *The Philokalia*, 1:163–98.
36. *Corpus Scriptorum Christianorum Orientalium* (Louvain: n.p., 1903–), 89.4–5 (trans. Veilleux, as cited by William Harmless, *Desert Christians: An Introduc-*

tion to the Literature of Early Monasticism (New York: Oxford Univ. Press, 2004), 118–19.
37. Note that the colony of hermits who lived in Sketis to the far north had no highly organized *Rule* like Pachomius's. Their norms of life were to simply follow the Gospels, the customs, and the wisdom of any experienced *abba*.
38. Harmless, *Desert Christians*, 115–16.
39. I borrow this phrase from the excellent introduction to desert spirituality by Roberta Bondi, *To Love as God Loves* (Philadelphia: Fortress, 1987).
40. A word of caution: Unconditional obedience to a spiritual leader and a tightly controlled community life have, at times, turned monasteries and churches into cults. Mind control, shame, and other forms of spiritual abuse can result from manipulation and a failure to test all community actions by the norms of Scripture.
41. Quoted by Lucien Regnault, *The Day-to-Day Life of the Desert Fathers in Fourth-Century Egypt* (trans. Etienne Poirier Jr.; Petersham, MA: St. Bedes Publication, 1999), 24. For a defense of the dignity of women and children in the desert against the view that the Desert Fathers were male chauvinists, see 24–28.
42. Elizabeth Clark, *Life of Melania the Younger: Introduction, Translation, and Commentary* (New York: Mellon, 1984).
43. All quotes by Palladius are taken from ibid., 141 and following.
44. *Sayings of the Desert Fathers* (trans. Benedicta Ward; Kalamazoo, MI: Cistercian Publications, 1975); "John the Dwarf," #36 (p. 93). The most complete biography on the life of John the Little is *The Holy Workshop of Virtue*, eds. Tim Vivian, Rowan Greer, and Maged S.A. Mikhail (Kalamazoo, MI: Cistercian Publications, 2010).
45. *Sayings of the Desert Fathers*, "John the Dwarf," #2 (p. 86).
46. Ibid., #11 (p. 87).
47. Ibid., #1 (pp. 85–86). In another version of the story by John Cassian (AD 360–435; *The Institutes* 4.24), the wood stays dry. But the main point about obedience remains the same.
48. Gary Burge, *Encounters with Jesus* (Ancient Context, Ancient Faith; Grand Rapids: Zondervan, 2010), see ch. 5 (pp. 95–110)
49. *Sayings of the Desert Fathers*, "John the Dwarf," #40 (pp. 93–94) (I rephrased parts of this translation for clarity).
50. *Sayings of the Desert Fathers*, "Moses the Ethiopian," #4 (p. 139).
51. Ibid., #6 (p. 139).
52. Quoted by William Harmless, *Desert Christians: An Introduction to the Literature of Early Monasticism* (New York: Oxford Univ. Press, 2004), 426.
53. *Sayings of the Desert Fathers*, Instruction #1 and 7 (pp. 141–42).
54. See Bradley Nassif, "The Poverty of Love," *Christianity Today* 52/5 (May 2008): 34–37; see www.ctlibrary.com/ct/2008/may/11.34.html.

Ancient Context, Ancient Faith

The Bible and the Land

Gary M. Burge

As the early church moved away from the original cultural setting of the Bible and found its home in the west, Christians lost touch with the ancient world of the Bible. Cultural habits, the particulars of landscape, even the biblical languages soon were unknown. And the cost was enormous: Christians began reading the Bible as foreigners and missing the original images and ideas that shaped a biblical worldview.

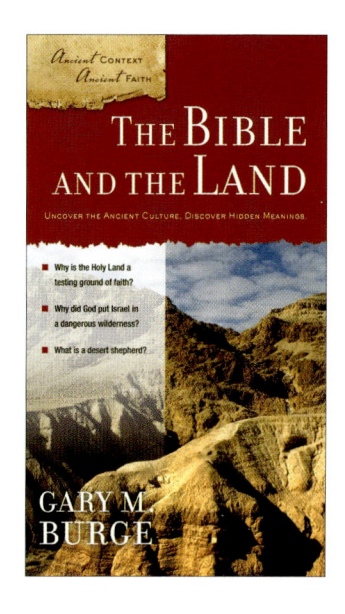

The Bible and the Land, by New Testament scholar Gary M. Burge, launches a multivolume series that explores how the culture of the biblical world is presupposed in story after story of the Bible. Using cultural anthropology, ancient literary sources, and a selective use of modern Middle Eastern culture, Burge reopens the ancient biblical story and urges us to look at them through new lenses. He explores primary motifs from the biblical landscape — geography, water, rock, bread, etc. — and applies them to vital stories from the Bible.

Each volume in the *Ancient Context, Ancient Faith* series is full color, rich with photographs, and in a travel size for convenient Bible study anywhere you go.

Available in stores and online!

ZONDERVAN
.com

Ancient Context, Ancient Faith

Jesus, the Middle Eastern Storyteller

Gary M. Burge

As the early church moved away from the original cultural setting of the Bible and found its home in the West, Christians lost touch with the ancient world of the Bible. Cultural habits, the particulars of landscape, even the biblical languages soon were unknown. And the cost was enormous: Christians began reading the Bible as foreigners and missing the original images and ideas that shaped a biblical worldview.

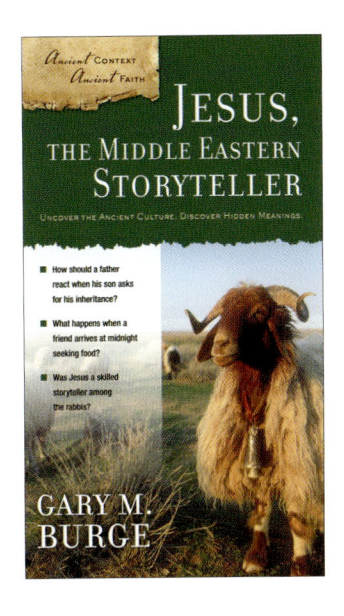

Jesus, the Middle Eastern Storyteller, by New Testament scholar Gary M. Burge, explains that Jesus lived in a storytelling culture that was completely unlike the modern world. When we imagine Jesus' teaching in his own time and place, we cannot use profiles of teachers from our own setting to understand the nature of his work. Jesus' world was different. Burge explains the parables as they have been rarely explained before. He brings new insight to Jesus' view of God and his understanding of the life of discipleship.

Each volume in the *Ancient Context, Ancient Faith* series is full-color, rich with photographs, and in a travel size for convenient Bible study anywhere you go.

Available in stores and online!

ZONDERVAN®
.com

Ancient Context, Ancient Faith

Encounters with Jesus

Gary M. Burge

Do you sometimes feel like an "untouchable"? Have you ever been ashamed to say, "You don't know what I've done, how unethical I've been, how many bad decisions I've made, how many times I've shaken my fist at God"?

If so, you're not alone.

Thankfully, author Gary M. Burge has a message for you, and others like you: Jesus wants to encounter you, just as you are. When Burge reexamined Jesus' biblical encounters with people — being careful to view them in their unique historical context — he emerged with fresh, powerful insights about how Jesus interacted with people then, and still does today.

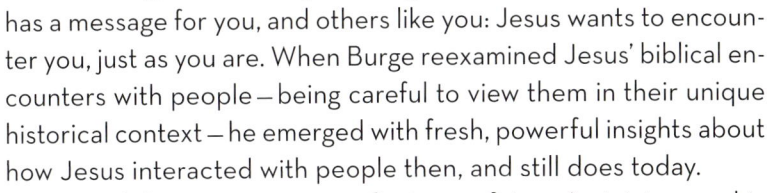

"One of the more surprising features of Jesus' ministry was his willingness to have personal encounters with people," he writes. "In fact, what is unique about the gospels are the unexpected stories that detailed Jesus' regular interruptions." Such "interruptions" came in the form of people from all walks of life — young and old, rich and poor, sick and healthy, those riddled with sin or saddled by self-righteousness. "No situation or condition will impede Jesus' approach," Burge writes. "All are welcome."

Encounters with Jesus is a book that will be read, reread, and recommended to friends and family alike because its message is sorely needed today: "Jesus took time for people who thought they were invisible ... this is a relief to those of us who are imperfect."

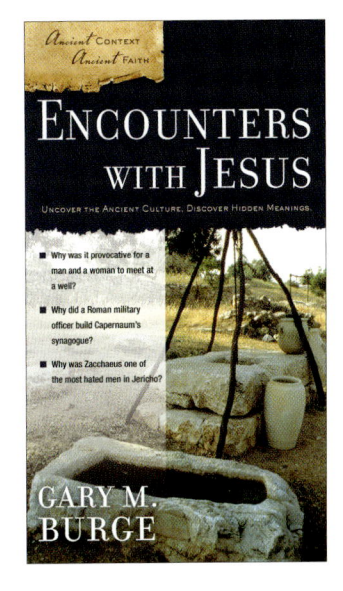

Available in stores and online!

ZONDERVAN®
.com